Bible 11
Teacher's Guide

CONTENTS

Author: **Alpha Omega Publications**
Editor: Alan Christopherson, M.S.

Alpha Omega Publications®

804 N. 2nd Ave. E., Rock Rapids, IA 51246-1759

OVERVIEW

BIBLE

Curriculum Overview
Grades 1–12

Bible LIFEPAC Overview

	Grade 1	Grade 2	Grade 3
LIFEPAC 1	GOD CREATED ALL THINGS • God created day and night • God created land and sea • God created plants and animals • God created people	WHO AM I? • God made us • God loves me • God helps me • God helped Daniel	WHY AM I HERE? • I love and obey God • I praise God • I worship God • I serve God
LIFEPAC 2	GOD LOVES HIS CHILDREN • God cared for Shadrach, Meshach, and Abednego • God cared for Joash and Esther • God cares for his Children • God's children love Him	THE STORY OF MOSES • The early life of Moses • Life in Midian • Moses returns to Egypt • Life in the desert	THE LIFE OF JESUS • Mary and Joseph • Jesus in the Temple • Jesus teaches and saves • Jesus dies and lives again
LIFEPAC 3	WE CAN PRAY • We can ask and thank God • We can pray God's special prayer • God listens to us • We listen to God	GOD AND YOU • God is great • God keeps his promises • You should obey God • God rewards his people	GOD'S PLAN FOR JOSEPH • The dream of Joseph • Joseph and his brothers • Joseph in Egypt • God watched over Joseph
LIFEPAC 4	GOD WANTS YOU TO BE GOOD • Jesus says love God • God says to love others • You show your love • God says to love yourself	HOW THE BIBLE CAME • Moses and the Prophets • David and Solomon • The Apostles and Paul • Bible translators	YOU CAN USE THE BIBLE • The books of the Bible • How to read and study the Bible • How to find verses • How to memorize verses
LIFEPAC 5	OLD TESTAMENT STORIES • Joseph, Elijah, Johathan, and David • Miriam and Deborah • A rich woman and her son • Ishmael and Mephibosheth	DAVID'S SLING • David with the sheep • David and the prophet • David and Saul • David and the giant	GOD CARES FOR HIS PEOPLE • God's love for people • God guides people • God protects people • God blesses people
LIFEPAC 6	GOD'S PROMISE • God's Old Testament promises • God's promises kept • The birth of the Promised One • The life of the Promised One	GOD IS EVERYWHERE • Understanding the beginning • Understanding God • The creation • God's will	THE BIBLE, GOD'S WORD • The writers of God's Word • God's Word is preserved • God's Word changes lives • Promises of God's Word
LIFEPAC 7	JESUS, OUR SAVIOR • Jesus taught the people • Jesus healed the people • Jesus saves the people • Jesus will come again	THE STORY OF JOSEPH • Joseph as a boy at home • The worship of Joseph • Joseph in Egypt • Joseph and the famine	ARCHEOLOGY AND THE BIBLE • The search for treasure • Clues from old stories • Explaining the puzzles • Joining the search
LIFEPAC 8	GOD CALLS MISSIONARIES • The woman at the well • Stephen and Paul • Missionaries today • God calls missionaries	GOD AND THE FAMILY • The first family • Abraham's family • Happy families • God's promise to children	THE NEED FOR FRIENDS • We need love • We need friendship • God commands our love • Love for others
LIFEPAC 9	NEW TESTAMENT STORIES • Lazarus, Thomas, Stephen • Mary, Anna, Lydia • Children of the New Testament • Jesus and the Children	GOD MADE THE NATIONS • The people of Babel • God's judgement at Babel • The new nation • Our big world	GOD'S PEOPLE HELP OTHERS • All people are created by God • God loves me • God's love to others • God is my Father
LIFEPAC 10	GOD GAVE YOU MANY GIFTS • God created all things • God loves His children • God gave us His Word • God gave us His Son	GOD, HIS WORD, AND YOU • God as our father • The word of God • Life with God • Belonging to God	GOD'S WORD, JESUS, AND YOU • God speaks to Man • Writers of the Word • Jesus and the Word • God's family

Grade 4	Grade 5	Grade 6	
HOW CAN I LIVE FOR GOD? • Peter found Jesus • Peter Fished for Men • To be born into God's family • To be fruitful through the Spirit	HOW OTHERS LIVED FOR GOD • Fellow-laborers with God • Abraham, a man of faith • Servants of God • Co-workers with God	FROM CREATION TO MOSES • Creation • The Flood • Abraham and his descendants • Moses and the Law	LIFEPAC 1
GOD'S KNOWLEDGE • Knowledge to create • Learning God's knowledge • The benefits of God's knowledge • Using God's knowledge	ANGELS • Characteristics of Angels • Kinds of Angels • The ministry of Angels • Angels in the life of Jesus	FROM JOSHUA TO SAMUEL • Conquest and division of the land • The death of Joshua • The Judges of Israel • Ruth, Naomi, and Boaz	LIFEPAC 2
SAUL BEGINS TO LIVE FOR GOD • Saul persecutes the Christians • God changes Saul • Saul preaches about Jesus • Paul belongs to Christ	THE PRESENCE OF GOD • Everywhere as God • Everywhere as a person • In the lives of people • In my life	THE KINGDOM OF ISRAEL • Samuel and Saul • The reign of David • The reign of Solomon • The books of poetry	LIFEPAC 3
THE BIBLE AND ME • Reading and learning the Bible • Thinking about the Bible • Memorizing the Bible • Living the Bible way	BIBLE METHODS AND STRUCTURE • One book with many parts • Books of history • Books of poetry and prophecy • Books of the New Testament	THE DIVIDED KINGDOM • From Jeroboam to Captivity • Prophets of Judah and Israel • From Hezekiah to Captivity • Prophets of remaining kingdom	LIFEPAC 4
GOD CARES FOR US • The Twenty-third Psalm • Jesus and the sheep • David as a shepherd • Daniel as a helper	THE CHRISTIAN IN THE WORLD • Instruction and correction • Learning correct behavior • Relationships at school • Relationships in the world	CAPTIVITY AND RESTORATION • The prophets of the captivity • The returns from exile • The prophets of the Restoration • Creation to Restoration	LIFEPAC 5
HOW CAN I KNOW GOD EXISTS • God's plan for the Jews • A Jewish Savior • Man searches for God • Man needs God	PROVING WHAT WE BELIEVE • The Bible is God's Word • Evidence from the Bible • Evidence from history and science • Knowing that Christ arose	THE LIFE OF JESUS • Birth and background • The first years of ministry • The latter years of ministry • The death and Resurrection	LIFEPAC 6
OLD TESTAMENT GEOGRAPHY • Bible Geography • Description of the Land • Abram's Nomadic Life • Abraham's Descendants	MISSIONARY JOURNEYS OF PAUL • Paul's background • Paul's missionary journeys • The Jerusalem Council • Paul's last years	THE FOLLOWERS OF JESUS • The disciples of Jesus • The friends of Jesus • Miracles of Jesus • The message of Jesus	LIFEPAC 7
GOD–GIVEN WORTH • Who Am I? • God is my Creator • God is my Father • Knowing God's Love	GOD CREATED MAN FOR ETERNITY • Preparing for eternity • Christ is our Judge • The judgment of the Christian • The judgment of the unsaved	THE APOSTLE PAUL • Paul's background and conversion • Paul's missionary journeys • Paul's letters to churches • Paul's letters to people	LIFEPAC 8
WITNESSING FOR JESUS • Loving God and Others • Following Jesus • Knowing who Jesus is • Following Paul's Example	AUTHORITY AND LAW • God is the source of law • The model of law • The authority of the family • Our authority of government	HEBREWS AND GENERAL EPISTLES • The book of Hebrews • James and 1st and 2nd Peter • The three Johns • The book of Jude	LIFEPAC 9
GOD'S WAY IS PERFECT • Seeking Knowledge • Science & Geography • Living God's Way • Loving God's Way	ANGELS, THE BIBLE, LIVING FOR GOD • Presence of God and Angels • Understanding the Bible • Areas of service • The order of authority	REVELATION AND REVIEW • The Lord Jesus in Revelation • End-time events • Old Testament review • New Testament review	LIFEPAC 10

Bible LIFEPAC Overview

	Grade 7	Grade 8	Grade 9
LIFEPAC 1	WORSHIP • The nature of worship • Old Testament worship • New Testament worship • True worship	PRAYER • Organization of the Lord's Prayer • Purpose of the Lord's Prayer • History of prayer • Practical use of prayer	THE NEW TESTAMENT • Inter-Testamental period • Pharisees and Sadducees • New Testament themes • New Testament events
LIFEPAC 2	MANKIND • The origin of man • The fall of man • The re-creation of man • The mission of man	SIN AND SALVATION • The nature of sin • The need for salvation • How to receive salvation • The results of salvation	THE GOSPELS • Matthew • Mark • Luke • John
LIFEPAC 3	THE ATTRIBUTES OF GOD • God's nature of love • God's expression of love • The mercy of God • The grace of God	ATTRIBUTES OF GOD • God's justice • God's immutability • God's eternal nature • God's love	THE ACTS OF THE APOSTLES • The writer • The purpose • Pentecost • Missions
LIFEPAC 4	FULFILLED PROPHECIES OF CHRIST • Method of the First Advent • Purpose of the First Advent • The Messiah foretold • Fulfillment of the Messiah	EARLY CHURCH LEADERS • The early church • The church of the Middle Ages • The Renaissance • The Reformation	THE PAULINE EPISTLES • Paul as a person • The early epistles • Prison epistles • The later epistles
LIFEPAC 5	LIVING THE BALANCED LIFE • The Father's gift of life • Man's deception • Fellowship with the Savior • The life of the Spirit	EARLY CHURCH HISTORY • The Roman Empire • The background of the Jews • The ministry of Jesus • The Jerusalem church	GENERAL EPISTLES • James • First and Second Peter • First, Second, and Third John • Hebrews and Jude
LIFEPAC 6	THE PSALMS • The history of the Psalms • Types of Psalms • Hebrew poetry • Psalm 100	THE EARLY CHURCHES • The church at Antioch • The missionary journeys • The Jerusalem Conference • New Testament churches	THE REVELATION OF JESUS CHRIST • The seven churches • The seven seals and trumpets • The seven signs and plagues • The seven judgments and wonders
LIFEPAC 7	THE LIFE OF CHRIST: PART ONE • Early life of Christ • Christ's ministry begins • The early Judean ministry • The early Galilean ministry	THE BOOK OF PROVERBS • Literary forms and outline • Objectives and purposes • Influence on the New Testament • Key themes	JOB AND SUFFERING • The scenes of Job • Attitudes toward suffering • Christ's suffering on earth • The victory of Christ's suffering
LIFEPAC 8	THE LIFE OF CHRIST: PART TWO • The public ministry in Galilee • The private ministry in Galilee • The Judean ministry • The Perean ministry	TODAY'S PROBLEMS • Guidance for behavior • Characteristics of friendship • Studying effectively • Finding God's will	HOW TO SHARE CHRIST • Personal evangelism • Outreach to others • Personal and family missions • Assisting a missionary
LIFEPAC 9	THE LIFE OF CHRIST: PART THREE • The public Jerusalem ministry • The private Jerusalem ministry • The Crucifixion • The Resurrection	UNDERSTANDING PARENTS • Human parents • Biblical parents • Children's responsibility • Parents and children as a team	GOD'S WILL FOR MY LIFE • The desire of the heart • The Word and work of God • Importance of goals • The use of talents
LIFEPAC 10	IN SUMMARY • The plan of God • Man's history • The Savior's solution • Worship of Christ	WALKING WITH GOD • Prayer and salvation • The attributes of God • The early church leaders • Christian living	THE WALK WITH CHRIST • Background of the New Testament • The Epistles and Revelation • The importance of suffering • God's will for my life

Grade 10	Grade 11	Grade 12	
CREATION TO ABRAHAM • The six days of creation • The fall of man • Noah and his descendants • Nations of the earth	THE FAITHFULNESS OF GOD • Affirmation of God's faithfulness • Nature of God's faithfulness • Manifestations of God's faithfulness • Implications of God's faithfulness	KNOWING YOURSELF • Your creation by God • Interacting with others • A child and servant of God • Your personal skills	LIFEPAC 1
ABRAHAM TO MOSES • Abraham's call and promise • The covenant with Isaac • The life of Jacob • Joseph and his family	ROMANS: PART ONE • The Roman Empire and Church • The book of Romans • Paul's message to the Romans • Sin and salvation in Romans	CHRISTIAN MINISTRIES • Christian ministry defined • Church related ministries • Other ministries • A ministry as a career	LIFEPAC 2
EXODUS AND WANDERINGS • The journey to Sinai • The giving of the Law • Numbering the people • The book of Deuteronomy	ROMANS: PART TWO • The chosen of God • Service and submission • From sin to salvation • The victory of salvation	CHOOSING A CHRISTIAN MINISTRY • Where to look for a ministry • What to look for in a ministry • How to look for a ministry • Choosing a ministry for a career	LIFEPAC 3
ISRAEL IN CANAAN • Preparing for battle • The fight for the land • Dividing the land • The death of Joshua	THE DOCTRINE OF JESUS CHRIST • Identity and incarnation of Christ • The individuality of Christ • Christ's work on the Cross • Christ's work after the Cross	GODHEAD • Old Testament view • New Testament view • Historical Perspectives • Faith and man's relationship	LIFEPAC 4
THE JUDGES AND SPIRITUAL DECLINE • Background of Judges • History of the Judges • Examples of spiritual decay • Ruth and redemption	THE NATION OF ISRAEL • The covenant with Abraham • Israel as a nation • Old Testament archaeology • New Testament archaeology	ATTRIBUTES OF GOD • The Holiness of God • The Goodness of God • Holiness and the believer • Goodness and the Creation	LIFEPAC 5
THE KINGDOM • Samuel and Saul • David • Solomon • Hebrew poetry	HISTORY OF THE CANON • Revelation and inspiration • Illumination and interpretation • Authority of the Bible • Formation of the Bible	THE EPISTLES OF JAMES • James the man • The message of James • John the man • The message of John's epistles	LIFEPAC 6
THE DIVIDED KINGDOM • Jeroboam to Ahab • Ahab to Jehu • Jehu to Assyrian captivity • Prophets of the period	FRIENDSHIP, DATING, AND MARRIAGE • Meaning and role of friendship • Perspectives of dating • Principles of relationships • The structure of marriage	DANIEL • A man of conviction • An interpreter of dreams • A watchman in prayer • A man of visions	LIFEPAC 7
THE REMAINING KINGDOM • The time of Hezekiah • Manasseh to Josiah • Jehoahaz to the exile • Prophets of the period	THE PURSUIT OF HAPPINESS • Solomon's succession • Solomon's prosperity • Solomon's fall • Solomon's reflection	COMPARATIVE RELIGIONS • Elements of Christianity • The validity of Christian faith • World religions • The occult	LIFEPAC 8
THE CAPTIVITY • Prophets of the period • Jeremiah • Ezekiel • Daniel	ANSWERS FOR AGNOSTICS • Integrity of the Bible • Doctrines of the Bible • Interpretation of the Bible • Application of the Bible	WISDOM FOR TODAY'S YOUTH • Life and character of David • Life and riches of Solomon • Psalms and Proverbs • The Bible and literature	LIFEPAC 9
THE RESTORATION • First return from exile • The Jews preserved • Second return from exile • Haggai, Zechariah, and Malachi	GOD, HIS WORD, AND THE CHRISTIAN • The uniqueness of the Bible • History of Israel • God revealed in the Bible • Principles for living	PRACTICAL CHRISTIAN LIVING • Christian fundamentals • Growing in Christian maturity • A ministry for Christ • A testimony for Christ	LIFEPAC 10

MANAGEMENT

STRUCTURE OF THE LIFEPAC CURRICULUM

The LIFEPAC curriculum is conveniently structured to provide one teacher handbook containing teacher support material with answer keys and ten student worktexts for each subject at grade levels two through twelve. The worktext format of the LIFEPACs allows the student to read the textual information and complete workbook activities all in the same booklet. The easy to follow LIFEPAC numbering system lists the grade as the first number(s) and the last two digits as the number of the series. For example, the Language Arts LIFEPAC at the 6th grade level, 5th book in the series would be LAN0605.

Each LIFEPAC is divided into 3 to 5 sections and begins with an introduction or overview of the booklet as well as a series of specific learning objectives to give a purpose to the study of the LIFEPAC. The introduction and objectives are followed by a vocabulary section which may be found at the beginning of each section at the lower levels, at the beginning of the LIFEPAC in the middle grades, or in the glossary at the high school level. Vocabulary words are used to develop word recognition and should not be confused with the spelling words introduced later in the LIFEPAC. The student should learn all vocabulary words before working the LIFEPAC sections to improve comprehension, retention, and reading skills.

Each activity or written assignment has a number for easy identification, such as 1.1. The first number corresponds to the LIFEPAC section and the number to the right of the decimal is the number of the activity.

Teacher checkpoints, which are essential to maintain quality learning, are found at various locations throughout the LIFEPAC. The teacher should check 1) neatness of work and penmanship, 2) quality of understanding (tested with a short oral quiz), 3) thoroughness of answers (complete sentences and paragraphs, correct spelling, etc.), 4) completion of activities (no blank spaces), and 5) accuracy of answers as compared to the answer key (all answers correct).

The self test questions are also number coded for easy reference. For example, 2.015 means that this is the 15th question in the self test of Section II. The first number corresponds to the LIFEPAC section, the zero indicates that it is a self test question, and the number to the right of the zero the question number.

The LIFEPAC test is packaged at the centerfold of each LIFEPAC. It should be removed and put aside before giving the booklet to the student for study.

Answer and test keys have the same numbering system as the LIFEPACs and appear at the back of this handbook. The student may be given access to the answer keys (not the test keys) under teacher supervision so that he can score his own work.

A thorough study of the Curriculum Overview by the teacher before instruction begins is essential to the success of the student. The teacher should become familiar with expected skill mastery and understand how these grade level skills fit into the overall skill development of the curriculum. The teacher should also preview the objectives that appear at the beginning of each LIFEPAC for additional preparation and planning.

TEST SCORING and GRADING

Answer keys and test keys give examples of correct answers. They convey the idea, but the student may use many ways to express a correct answer. The teacher should check for the essence of the answer, not for the exact wording. Many questions are high level and require thinking and creativity on the part of the student. Each answer should be scored based on whether or not the main idea written by the student matches the model example. "Any Order" or "Either Order" in a key indicates that no particular order is necessary to be correct.

Most self tests and LIFEPAC tests at the lower elementary levels are scored at 1 point per answer; however, the upper levels may have a point system awarding 2 to 5 points for various answers or questions. Further, the total test points will vary; they may not always equal 100 points. They may be 78, 85, 100, 105, etc.

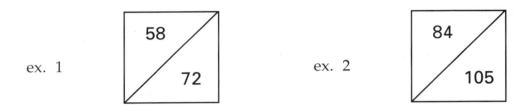

ex. 1   58 / 72   ex. 2   84 / 105

A score box similar to ex.1 above is located at the end of each self test and on the front of the LIFEPAC test. The bottom score, 72, represents the total number of points possible on the test. The upper score, 58, represents the number of points your student will need to receive an 80% or passing grade. If you wish to establish the exact percentage that your student has achieved, find the total points of his correct answers and divide it by the bottom number (in this case 72.) For example, if your student has a point total of 65, divide 65 by 72 for a grade of 90%. Referring to ex. 2, on a test with a total of 105 possible points, the student would have to receive a minimum of 84 correct points for an 80% or passing grade. If your student has received 93 points, simply divide the 93 by 105 for a percentage grade of 89%. Students who receive a score below 80% should review the LIFEPAC and retest using the appropriate Alternate Test found in the Teacher's Guide.

The following is a guideline to assign letter grades for completed LIFEPACs based on a maximum total score of 100 points.

LIFEPAC Test = 60% of the Total Score (or percent grade)
Self Test   = 25% of the Total Score (average percent of self tests)
Reports   = 10% or 10* points per LIFEPAC
Oral Work   = 5% or 5* points per LIFEPAC
*Determined by the teacher's subjective evaluation of the student's daily work.

Example:

LIFEPAC Test Score	=	92%	92 x .60	=	55 points
Self Test Average	=	90%	90 x .25	=	23 points
Reports				=	8 points
Oral Work				=	4 points

TOTAL POINTS	=	90 points

Grade Scale based on point system:

100	–	94	=	A
93	–	86	=	B
85	–	77	=	C
76	–	70	=	D
Below		70	=	F

TEACHER HINTS and STUDYING TECHNIQUES

LIFEPAC Activities are written to check the level of understanding of the preceding text. The student may look back to the text as necessary to complete these activities; however, a student should never attempt to do the activities without reading (studying) the text first. Self tests and LIFEPAC tests are never open book tests.

Language arts activities (skill integration) often appear within other subject curriculum. The purpose is to give the student an opportunity to test his skill mastery outside of the context in which it was presented.

Writing complete answers (paragraphs) to some questions is an integral part of the LIFEPAC Curriculum in all subjects. This builds communication and organization skills, increases understanding and retention of ideas, and helps enforce good penmanship. Complete sentences should be encouraged for this type of activity. Obviously, single words or phrases do not meet the intent of the activity, since multiple lines are given for the response.

Review is essential to student success. Time invested in review where review is suggested will be time saved in correcting errors later. Self tests, unlike the section activities, are closed book. This procedure helps to identify weaknesses before they become too great to overcome. Certain objectives from self tests are cumulative and test previous sections; therefore, good preparation for a self test must include all material studied up to that testing point.

The following procedure checklist has been found to be successful in developing good study habits in the LIFEPAC curriculum.

1. Read the introduction and Table of Contents.
2. Read the objectives.
3. Recite and study the entire vocabulary (glossary) list.
4. Study each section as follows:
    a. Read the introduction and study the section objectives.
    b. Read all the text for the entire section, but answer none of the activities.
    c. Return to the beginning of the section and memorize each vocabulary word and definition.
    d. Reread the section, complete the activities, check the answers with the answer key, correct all errors, and have the teacher check.
    e. Read the self test but do not answer the questions.
    f. Go to the beginning of the first section and reread the text and answers to the activities up to the self test you have not yet done.
    g. Answer the questions to the self test without looking back.
    h. Have the self test checked by the teacher.
    i. Correct the self test and have the teacher check the corrections.
    j. Repeat steps a–i for each section.

5. Use the SQ3R* method to prepare for the LIFEPAC test.
6. Take the LIFEPAC test as a closed book test.
7. LIFEPAC tests are administered and scored under direct teacher supervision. Students who receive scores below 80% should review the LIFEPAC using the SQ3R* study method and take the Alternate Test located in the Teacher Handbook. The final test grade may be the grade on the Alternate Test or an average of the grades from the original LIFEPAC test and the Alternate Test.

   *SQ3R: **S**can the whole LIFEPAC.
        Question yourself on the objectives.
        Read the whole LIFEPAC again.
        Recite through an oral examination.
        Review weak areas.

GOAL SETTING and SCHEDULES

Each school must develop its own schedule, because no single set of procedures will fit every situation. The following is an example of a daily schedule that includes the five LIFEPAC subjects as well as time slotted for special activities.

Possible Daily Schedule

8:15	–	8:25	Pledges, prayer, songs, devotions, etc.
8:25	–	9:10	Bible
9:10	–	9:55	Language Arts
9:55	–	10:15	Recess (juice break)
10:15	–	11:00	Mathematics
11:00	–	11:45	Social Studies
11:45	–	12:30	Lunch, recess, quiet time
12:30	–	1:15	Science
1:15	–		Drill, remedial work, enrichment*

*Enrichment: Computer time, physical education, field trips, fun reading, games and puzzles, family business, hobbies, resource persons, guests, crafts, creative work, electives, music appreciation, projects.

Basically, two factors need to be considered when assigning work to a student in the LIFEPAC curriculum.

The first is time. An average of 45 minutes should be devoted to each subject, each day. Remember, this is only an average. Because of extenuating circumstances a student may spend only 15 minutes on a subject one day and the next day spend 90 minutes on the same subject.

The second factor is the number of pages to be worked in each subject. A single LIFEPAC is designed to take 3 to 4 weeks to complete. Allowing about 3-4 days for LIFEPAC introduction, review, and tests, the student has approximately 15 days to complete the LIFEPAC pages. Simply take the number of pages in the LIFEPAC, divide it by 15 and you will have the number of pages that must be completed on a daily basis to keep the student on schedule. For example, a LIFEPAC containing 45 pages will require 3 completed pages per day. Again, this is only an average. While working a 45 page LIFEPAC, the student may complete only 1 page the first day if the text has a lot of activities or reports, but go on to complete 5 pages the next day.

Long range planning requires some organization. Because the traditional school year originates in the early fall of one year and continues to late spring of the following year, a calendar should be devised that covers this period of time. Approximate beginning and completion dates can be noted on the calendar as well as special occasions such as holidays, vacations and birthdays. Since each LIFEPAC takes 3-4 weeks or eighteen days to complete, it should take about 180 school days to finish a set of ten LIFEPACs. Starting at the beginning school date, mark off eighteen school days on the calendar and that will become the targeted completion date for the first LIFEPAC. Continue marking the calendar until you have established dates for the remaining nine LIFEPACs making adjustments for previously noted holidays and vacations. If all five subjects are being used, the ten established target dates should be the same for the LIFEPACs in each subject.

FORMS

The sample weekly lesson plan and student grading sheet forms are included in this section as teacher support materials and may be duplicated at the convenience of the teacher.

The student grading sheet is provided for those who desire to follow the suggested guidelines for assignment of letter grades found on page 3 of this section. The student's self test scores should be posted as percentage grades. When the LIFEPAC is completed the teacher should average the self test grades, multiply the average by .25 and post the points in the box marked self test points. The LIFEPAC percentage grade should be multiplied by .60 and posted. Next, the teacher should award and post points for written reports and oral work. A report may be any type of written work assigned to the student whether it is a LIFEPAC or additional learning activity. Oral work includes the student's ability to respond orally to questions which may or may not be related to LIFEPAC activities or any type of oral report assigned by the teacher. The points may then be totaled and a final grade entered along with the date that the LIFEPAC was completed.

The Student Record Book which was specifically designed for use with the Alpha Omega curriculum provides space to record weekly progress for one student over a nine week period as well as a place to post self test and LIFEPAC scores. The Student Record Books are available through the current Alpha Omega catalog; however, unlike the enclosed forms these books are not for duplication and should be purchased in sets of four to cover a full academic year.

WEEKLY LESSON PLANNER

Week of:

Subject	Subject	Subject	Subject

Monday

Subject	Subject	Subject	Subject

Tuesday

Subject	Subject	Subject	Subject

Wednesday

Subject	Subject	Subject	Subject

Thursday

Subject	Subject	Subject	Subject

Friday

WEEKLY LESSON PLANNER

Week of:

	Subject	Subject	Subject	Subject
Monday				
Tuesday	Subject	Subject	Subject	Subject
Wednesday	Subject	Subject	Subject	Subject
Thursday	Subject	Subject	Subject	Subject
Friday	Subject	Subject	Subject	Subject

Student Name _____   Year _____

Bible

LP #	Self Test Scores by Sections 1	2	3	4	5	Self Test Points	LIFEPAC Test	Oral Points	Report Points	Final Grade	Date
01											
02											
03											
04											
05											
06											
07											
08											
09											
10											

History & Geography

LP #	Self Test Scores by Sections 1	2	3	4	5	Self Test Points	LIFEPAC Test	Oral Points	Report Points	Final Grade	Date
01											
02											
03											
04											
05											
06											
07	94	92	93			93	95				
08	88	90	86			88	94				
09											
10											

Language Arts

LP #	Self Test Scores by Sections 1	2	3	4	5	Self Test Points	LIFEPAC Test	Oral Points	Report Points	Final Grade	Date
01											
02											
03											
04											
05											
06											
07											
08											
09											
10											

Student Name _____   Year _____

Mathematics

LP #	Self Test Scores by Sections 1	2	3	4	5	Self Test Points	LIFEPAC Test	Oral Points	Report Points	Final Grade	Date
01											
02											
03											
04											
05											
06											
07											
08											
09											
10											

Science

LP #	Self Test Scores by Sections 1	2	3	4	5	Self Test Points	LIFEPAC Test	Oral Points	Report Points	Final Grade	Date
01											
02											
03											
04											
05											
06											
07											
08											
09											
10											

Spelling / Electives

LP #	Self Test Scores by Sections 1	2	3	4	5	Self Test Points	LIFEPAC Test	Oral Points	Report Points	Final Grade	Date
01											
02											
03											
04											
05											
06											
07											
08											
09											
10											

N O T E S

U7

$$95 \times .7 = 66.5$$
$$93 \times .3 = \underline{28}$$
$$\underline{94}.5$$

U8

$$94 \times .7 = 65.8$$
$$88 \times .3 = \underline{26.4}$$
$$\underline{92}.2$$

93

INSTRUCTIONS FOR BIBLE

The LIFEPAC curriculum from grades two through twelve is structured so that the daily instructional material is written directly into the LIFEPACs. The student is encouraged to read and follow this instructional material in order to develop independent study habits. The teacher should introduce the LIFEPAC to the student, set a required completion schedule, complete teacher checks, be available for questions regarding both content and procedures, administer and grade tests, and develop additional learning activities as desired. Teachers working with several students may schedule their time so that students are assigned to a quiet work activity when it is necessary to spend instructional time with one particular student.

The Teacher Notes section of the handbook lists the required or suggested materials for the LIFEPACs and provides additional learning activities for the students. The materials section refers only to LIFEPAC materials and does not include materials which may be needed for the additional activities. Additional learning activities provide a change from the daily school routine, encourage the student's interest in learning and may be used as a reward for good study habits.

Materials Needed for LIFEPAC
> Required:

> Suggested:
> King James Version of the Bible
> Other versions of the Bible, if available and permitted
> Harrison, Everett F. (ed.). *Baker's Dictionary of Theology*. Grand Rapids, MI: Baker Book House, 1960.
> Ryrie, Charles Caldwell. *Biblical Theology of the New Testament*. Chicago: Moody Press, 1959.
> Smith, Hannah Whitall. *The God of All Comfort*. Chicago: Moody Press, 1956.

Extended Writing Assignment

Activity 2.28. Have students select an area in their lives in which God has shown His faithfulness and write a paragraph telling about a specific incident. Check paragraph for spelling, punctuation, and grammar. These papers may be shared with the class.

Additional Learning Activities
Section I The Affirmation of God's Faithfulness
1. If we are not faithful to God in the routine experiences of life, can we expect His faithfulness to us in times of special testing?
2. Does the fact that Christians suffer from sickness, accidents, and so forth take away from God's faithfulness to His children?
3. People often refer to the "patience of Job." Do you agree with this comparison? How do you think Job kept so much patience through all of his sufferings?
4. Using a dictionary or thesaurus, write as many synonyms as you can find for the word *faithfulness*.
5. Using a dictionary or thesaurus, write as many antonyms as you can find for the word *faithfulness*.
6. Look up the word *shepherd* in an encyclopedia (regular or Bible). Write a two-paragraph comparison on how the shepherd cares for his sheep and how the Good Shepherd cares for His children.
7. Look in a Bible concordance and count the number of verses that refer to the faithfulness of God. Select one you especially like and memorize it.

Section II The Nature of God's Faithfulness
1. Discuss the idea of the changing world we live in, the unreliability of people, and then stress the fact that God never changes. He is always there, ready to listen, and will never betray our confidence.
2. Discuss the God-like attributes which man possesses and compare the attributes shared by man and God. (Examples: Man can be "knowing" but God is all-knowing. Man can love, but God's love sent His only Son to die on a cross.)
3. See who can make the most words out of the word *faithfulness*. Plurals and proper nouns do not count.
4. Make a mural of two or three biblical scenes depicting the faithfulness of God to His people.
5. From Activity 2.20 select one of the ten verses as your favorite. Write it on an index card and put it where you will see it often during the week. Memorize it, and repeat it to yourself during the day when you believe Satan is trying to tempt you.

6. Hebrews 6:13 through 18 says, "And so, after he (Abraham) had patiently endured, he obtained the promise." Write 100 words on the need for patience in a Christian's life.

7. We have read that men make gods of money, power, or pleasure and that athletic ability, social popularity, and academic achievement can also become gods. Have you put any of these things above God in your life? Is He first in your heart today?

Section III The Manifestations of God's Faithfulness

1. Discuss some of the ways God showed His faithfulness to Noah, Abraham, Isaac, Jacob, and Joseph; to the prophets Daniel and Elijah; through Christ to the disciples; to the early church; to church leaders through the centuries; and to us today—individually and the church as a whole.

2. Discuss the ways in which man has failed God and is failing Him today.

3. What is the difference between a conditional promise and an unconditional promise?

4. Do we ever make a conditional promise to God? Should we?

5. Prepare a newspaper that gives examples of God's faithfulness. (Activity 1 may be discussed first as a background.) The newspaper could include an editorial page, letters to the editor (written by people who have experienced God's faithfulness—Daniel, etc.), sports page (with witnesses from Christian athletes—Tom Landry, A. J. Green, etc.), and even a society section.

6. Look up the duties of a mediator (as in labor unions, etc.) in a dictionary or encyclopedia. Compare this definition to Christ being a mediator between God and man.

7. Do you really believe Romans 8:28? Can you remember a time in your life when it seemed things were going badly, only to find later that God had been working for your benefit? Write about this experience and share it with the class. (Are you going through something right now that you cannot see its purpose? Put your faith to work and apply Romans 8:28 to this problem.)

8. What does the word *sacrifice* mean to you? Have you ever sacrificed anything you wanted very much in order that someone else could have what they wanted or needed? Did you sacrifice out of duty or love? Could your sacrifice ever be so deep that you would give your life for another?

Section IV The Implications of God's Faithfulness

1. How do we know God will not fail? (Through faith we believe the Bible, and we know He never has failed us in the past.)

2. Discuss ways that we can show our faithfulness to God. (through church attendance, tithing, prayer, Bible reading, and witnessing)

3. How can people tell if we are not faithful to God? (It will eventually show itself in our behavior.)

4. Do you believe a person saved late in life will receive the same reward in heaven as someone who has worked for the Lord many years?

5. Have the students interview various Christians and list examples of God's faithfulness to them. Try to get a good cross-section: new Christians, mature Christians, senior citizens, teenagers, ministers, laymen, and so forth. Some of these people will tell of God's faithfulness in spiritual matters, others in financial or physical affairs. Share these interviews with the class.

6. Make a list of what stewardship involves. Is it just our money?

7. Talk to someone who became a Christian later in life. What reasons did he give for waiting so long? Has he experienced any regret for the wasted years? Without using his name, share his experience with an unsaved friend you are praying for.

8. Make a list of your talents; then ask yourself if you are presently allowing God to use all your talents and time. Can He depend on you? Write a prayer of commitment and put it where you will see it every morning. Remember, you not only need God, He needs you. You are His only hands.

Additional Activity

The activity on the next page may be reproduced as a student worksheet.

Additional Activity, Answer Key

NAME	REFERENCE
1. Abel	Genesis 4:3–5
2. Enoch	Genesis 5:22–24
3. Noah	Genesis 6:14–22
4. Abraham	Genesis 12:1–4
5. Sarah	Genesis 21:1 and 2
6. Isaac	Genesis 27:26–40
7. Jacob	Genesis 48:1–22
8. Joseph	Genesis 50:24 and 25
9. Moses	Exodus 2:11–15
10. Rahab	Joshua 2:1–21
11. Gideon	Judges 6:11
12. Barak	Judges 4:6–24
13. Samson	Judges 12:24–31
14. David	1 Samuel chapters 16 and 17
15. Samuel	1 Samuel 7:9–14
16. Jephthah	Judges 11:1–29

FAITHFUL HEROES OF THE WORD OF GOD

In Hebrews chapter 11, God gave us a list of faithful heroes of the Old Testament. Make a list of the Old Testament believers mentioned in this passage of God's Word. Try to find at least fifteen men and women who acted by faith. Then, using a concordance, topical Bible, Bible handbook, Bible dictionary, or Bible encyclopedia, find and write the Old Testament references to these great men and women of God.

Name   **Reference**

1. _____   _____

2. _____   _____

3. _____   _____

4. _____   _____

5. _____   _____

6. _____   _____

7. _____   _____

8. _____   _____

9. _____   _____

10. _____   _____

11. _____   _____

12. _____   _____

13. _____   _____

14. _____   _____

15. _____   _____

Materials Needed for LIFEPAC

Required:

Suggested:
The Epistle of Romans in a modern translation or paraphrase
Bible handbook
Bible encyclopedia
Bible maps of the days of the early church
Newell, William R. *Romans Verse by Verse.* Chicago: Moody Press, 1938.

Extended Writing Assignment

This essay should be about 300 words in length. The student should describe in as much detail as possible the city of Rome. Check for descriptive detail rather than broad generalities. Check for use of descriptive terms, spelling, grammar, and sentence structure. A logical outline should be developed and followed by the student.

Additional Learning Activities
Section I Historical Background

1. Can an uneducated person still be a witness for Jesus Christ? (We do not have to understand it, but we can still give our personal testimony. The blind man said, "Once I was blind, but now I see.")
2. Can too much education "turn someone off"? (It depends on whether you talk down to them or use words they can understand.)
3. What place should higher education play in a Christian's life? (Get all you can, but have heart knowledge as well as head knowledge.)
4. Why was the Roman Empire a good place for Christianity to begin? (It had good roads and seaports, a good postal system, and a way to get information from one place to another.)
5. Do you think it was a good idea to allow the older and more experienced men to become the leaders of the church? Should we exclude new Christians from holding church offices? (They should be given jobs, but not leadership positions, until they have become established in the faith and learn the doctrine.)
6. Set up a newspaper, called the Roman Empire *Republic,* describing the time of Nero. Include headline stories of current events, an editorial page, letters to the editor, sports page, and even a society section (which could include an "advice" column). There could also be some feature stories covering well known personalities. This paper could be expanded as the study continues and would make an excellent tool for review at the end of the LIFEPAC.
7. Have a press conference with reporters interviewing Paul about all his experiences.
8. Arrange to take a tour through a Jewish synagogue.
9. Have a discussion comparing the way the Gospel was spread in Paul's day to the methods we use today.
10. Draw or find a picture showing the city of Rome during the time of the Roman Empire. Find examples of the houses, the buildings, and the temples. Use Bible encyclopedias or magazines.
11. Write a brief summary of the reign of the five emperors of Rome and what each accomplished.

Section II Paul's Epistle to the Romans

1. Second Corinthians 6:17 says, "Wherefore come out from among them and be ye separate." How should we be separate from the world? (An expression says, "We don't have to be *isolated from* the world but we can be *insulated against* the world.")
2. The LIFEPAC says the Holy Spirit commends the churches before administering any correction. Would this be a good idea for everyone to follow?
3. Would the hardships Paul experienced keep you from being a witness for Christ?
4. What is the difference between the mercy of God and the justice of God?
5. Have a courtroom scene. Have a sinner come before the court (judge), be pronounced guilty, and then have Jesus appear as the defense attorney saying He represents the accused. The sinner goes free. Use considerable Scripture in conversation.
6. Have a contest to see who can make the most words out of the word *propitiation*.
7. Read the salutation to Romans (1:1-17) in a modern translation. Then write it in your own words, as though you were writing a letter to a friend.
8. Write a short paragraph on how sin is like a cancer.

Section III The Way According to Romans

1. How would being an ambassador for Christ compare with being an ambassador for a country?
2. Are we responsible for Adam's sin?
3. If we confess our sins, how do we know they are forgiven?
   Do we always feel different?
4. Why did man live so much longer in the Old Testament days than today?
5. Is there a difference between being a Christian and living the abundant life?
6. Divide into small groups and discuss the question: "What part does man play in his own salvation?" Summarize and report to the class.
7. Using a thesaurus, see how many words the class can find for *believe*.
8. Have each student write the name of one person they would like to see won to Christ. Discuss the best way to witness and the verses to use. Have a moment of silent prayer concentrating on that particular person. Urge them to try to witness to that person during the next week and have members of the class pray for each other. Share the results with the class and report on the ideas for witnessing that worked and those that did not.
9. Write a short paragraph explaining in your own words the meaning of, "I am the way, the truth, and the life."
10. Begin a handy notebook with all the Scriptures given in this LIFEPAC so that you will have your witness references available at all times. By reviewing the notebook often, you may be able to commit these verses to memory.

Additional Activity

The activity on the next page may be reproduced as a student worksheet

Additional Activity, Answer Key

	EPISTLE	DATE	TO WHOM	FROM WHERE
1.	1 Thessalonians	51 A.D.	Thessalonians	Corinth
2.	2 Thessalonians	51 A.D.	Thessalonians	Corinth
3.	Galatians	52 A.D.	Galatians	Corinth (?)
4.	1 Corinthians	56 A.D.	Corinthians	Ephesus
5.	Romans	56 A.D.	Rome	Corinth
6.	2 Corinthians	57 A.D.	Corinthians	Philippi
7.	Ephesians	60 A.D.	Ephesus	Rome
8.	Colossians	60 A.D.	Colossians	Rome
9	Philemon	60 A.D.	Philemon	Rome
10.	Philippians	60 A.D.	Philippi	Rome
11.	1 Timothy	64 A.D.	Timothy	unknown
12.	Titus	65 A.D.	Titus	Ephesus (?)
13.	2 Timothy	67 A.D.	Timothy	Rome

PAUL'S EPISTLES

In addition to the Epistle to the Romans, God the Holy Spirit inspired the apostle Paul to write twelve other Epistles that are included in the New Testament canon. Using a topical Bible, a Bible dictionary, Bible handbook, or a Bible encyclopedia, identify the other Epistle written by Paul. List them in chronological order beginning with the first letter written. List the date the Epistle was written and to whom it was written. Keep this chart for future reference.

	EPISTLE	DATE	TO WHOM	FROM WHERE
1.				
2.				
3.				
4.				
5.				
6.				
7.				
8.				
9.				
10.				
11.				
12.				
13.				

Materials Needed for LIFEPAC
Required:

Suggested:
The Holy Bible, King James Version and
other versions as available and permitted
Maps of the city of Rome during the first
century A.D.
Maps of the Roman Empire and the biblical
lands of the first century A.D.

Extended Writing Assignment

The student is to write a four-page essay dealing with the circumstances under which a Christian may be required to deny civil law and authority. The background reading for this report should be done in Daniel chapter 3, and Acts 5:17–32. The student should recognize that as a Christian he has a responsibility to obey the laws of the land as indicated by Paul in Romans chapter 13. However, the student should also recognize that he has a greater responsibility to follow the higher and absolute law of God as revealed in God's Word. We can only violate man's law when we clearly have a higher law from God.

Additional Learning Activities
Section I Children of Choice

1. Discuss with students the role of Israel in the current era. Use Romans chapters 9–11 as a resource. Discuss whether God's plan for His Old Testament people will be fulfilled or if the body of Christ has become the recipient of these promises.
2. Discuss with students how the book of Romans fits into the whole tapestry of Paul's Epistles. Use a Bible handbook to determine the themes of the other letters. Emphasize how each Epistle was revealed by God to give His children the information they need to live for Christ.
3. Have a group of students make a chart or poster that shows the Old Testament passages in Romans chapters 9–11 either cited or referred to by the Apostle Paul. This poster may be displayed in the classroom after it is completed.
4. Have students divide into groups and debate the fairness of imputing to all mankind the sin of Adam. Use the Genesis account and Romans chapter 5, as background information.
5. Make a list of the specific sins mentioned in the Word of God. Use Romans chapter 1, Proverbs chapter 6, and Galatians chapter 5 as your sources. Identify these sins as to whether they are mental-attitude sins, sins of the tongue, or overt sins. You may wish to make this list into a poster for display in the classroom.
6. Make a chronological chart of the important events in the brief history of the modern state of Israel. A modern encyclopedia will be helpful in completing this activity.

Section II Principles in Practice

1. Discuss with students the use of spiritual gifts described in Romans chapter 12. Find if everyone has a gift, if some have more than one, and what is required on the part of the believer in order for his gift or gifts to be used by the Lord.
2. Assign to each member of a small group one of the final chapters of the book of Romans. Have each student compose an outline for that chapter. Bring the group together to compile a master outline of these chapters of Romans.

3. In small groups, use role-playing to act out a witnessing situation. Have one student be the believer and another be the unbeliever. Have the students use only verses from the Romans Epistle to share the Gospel. Following each encounter, have the other students observe and evaluate the procedure.

4. Write out your own testimony. If you have previously given your testimony to a group of people, revise it in light of what you have learned from the study of Romans. Use verses from the Epistle to the Romans to tell of what your God has accomplished on your behalf.

5. Make a list of those things that are often deemed as Christian conduct. Then, using a concordance, try to find Scriptures that support these scruples. If no Scripture can be found, revise the list until you have true biblical principles for living the Christian life.

Section III Roman Victory

1. Discuss the concept of victory. How can we claim a victory won by another? What are the spoils of victory in Christ?

2. Using the Scripture required for memorization in this LIFEPAC, have a Scripture Memory Bee. Use a double elimination if the group is small.

3. Have a group of students make a list of things that are distractions in the Christian life. This list may also include those things that tend to defeat the believer. After the list is complete, find biblical passages and promises that counteract these distractions. These may be made into a poster for classroom display.

4. Have a group of students produce a short skit or play that shows a person in trouble and hard times. Have the other students offer him advice and help. Have the last friend give the correct biblical view of problems. Give the students extra credit if they realize this skit is the story of Job revised.

5. Begin making a promise notebook with the promises for Christian living from the book of Romans. Be sure to include only those promises that apply to you as a Christian. Write the entire verse in your promise notebook.

6. You have studied the theme of the Epistle to the Romans in this LIFEPAC. Using a Bible handbook, dictionary, or encyclopedia, find the theme of the remaining Epistles
of Paul. Also, arrange these letters in their correct chronological order, with the theme written beside them. Memorize these themes if possible.

Additional Activity
The activity on the next page may be reproduced as a student worksheet.

Additional Activity, Answer Key
Any student-developed chapter titles will meet the requirements of this activity as long as they summarize the essence of the chapter in a reasonable manner.

PAUL'S EPISTLE TO THE ROMANS

One interesting way to learn an entire book of the Bible is to write and then memorize chapter titles. You make up the titles in your own words and therefore memorize your own thoughts and ideas rather than those of someone else. You have studied the author's outline of Romans. Now write your own titles for each chapter. Memorize these titles and recite them before the class if your teacher allows.

Romans chapter 1 _____

Romans chapter 2 _____

Romans chapter 3 _____

Romans chapter 4 _____

Romans chapter 5 _____

Romans chapter 6 _____

Romans chapter 7 _____

Romans chapter 8 _____

Romans chapter 9 _____

Romans chapter 10 _____

Romans chapter 11 _____

Romans chapter 12 _____

Romans chapter 13 _____

Romans chapter 14 _____

Romans chapter 15 _____

Romans chapter 16 _____

Materials Needed for LIFEPAC:

Required:

Suggested:
Bible, King James Version
Other versions as available and permitted
Martin, Alfred and Dorothy. *The Lord Jesus Christ*. Chicago: Moody Press, 1973.
A personal Bible-study guide.
Ryrie, Charles C. "Jesus Christ the Lord," *A Survey of Bible Doctrine*. Chicago: Moody Press, 1972.
McDowell, Josh. *More Than a Carpenter*. Wheaton, IL: Tyndale House, 1977.

Extended Writing Assignment

The student is to write a two- or three-page report on the current ministry of the Lord Jesus. The paper is to be practical in nature and tell how the student depends upon Christ to be his High Priest, Intercessor, and Advocate. Additional resources should be used. Check for a logical outline, correct spelling and grammar, and clear sentence structure.

Additional Learning Activities
Section I The Person of Jesus Christ
1. In what ways does Jesus Christ differ from all other religious leaders?
2. How does the identity of Jesus Christ affect our salvation?
3. What is the relationship of Jesus Christ to the heavenly Father and the Holy Spirit?
4. How can Jesus Christ be fully God and fully man?
5. Was Jesus Christ not able to sin or able not to sin?
6. In what ways can we not be like Jesus Christ, and in what ways should we become like Him?
7. Conduct a debate between members of the group who assume various erroneous viewpoints of Jesus Christ and those who defend the biblical viewpoint.
8. Perform a drama depicting the debate at the Chalcedonian Council, along with its conclusion over the two natures of Jesus Christ.
9. Perform a drama depicting the Son of God volunteering to leave heaven and become a man.
10. Perform a drama depicting some incident in the life of Jesus that demonstrates His deity.
11. Interview many different kinds of people, asking them their opinions about Jesus Christ.
12. Write a first-century newspaper article about Jesus reporting an imaginary interview with one of His disciples.
13. Do a Bible study on some names and titles of Jesus Christ not explained in this LIFEPAC.
14. Write a first-century newspaper article reporting the birth of Jesus.
15. Write a defense of the virgin birth of Jesus Christ.
16. Write a defense of the deity of Jesus Christ.
17. List instances in the life of Jesus in which He exercised His divine attributes. Identify the attributes involved.

18. Identify Old Testament types or symbols of the person of Jesus Christ, describing what they indicate about Him.
19. Describe the unique emphasis and contribution of each of the four Gospels concerning Jesus Christ.
20. Write an essay on, "What the person of Jesus Christ means to me."
21. Write a prayer of praise for the person of Jesus Christ.

Section II The Work of Jesus Christ

1. What comparisons and contrasts can be made between the work of Christ in creation and His work in salvation?
2. Who is responsible for the death of Jesus Christ?
3. How does the Resurrection of Jesus Christ affect our Christian lives?
4. How should the return of Jesus Christ affect the way we live?
5. What has Jesus Christ done that no other religious leaders have done?
6. Perform a drama depicting some incident involving Christ as the Angel of the Lord.
7. Perform a drama depicting the trial of Jesus Christ.
8. Perform a drama depicting the Resurrection of Jesus Christ and the events surrounding it.
9. Perform a drama depicting some aspect of the present ministry of Christ in the life of a Christian.
10. Identify Old Testament types of symbols of the work of Jesus Christ.
11. List the Old Testament prophecies concerning some aspect of the work of Jesus Christ.
12. Summarize what you can know about Jesus Christ from the Old Testament alone.
13. Describe the symbolism of the sacrifices in Leviticus chapters 1–7 as types of the death of Jesus Christ.
14. Write a first-century newspaper article reporting some miracle of Jesus.
15. Write a first-century newspaper article reporting the trial and Crucifixion of Jesus.
16. Write an essay entitled, "What the Death of Christ Means to Me."
17. Write a defense of the substitutionary nature of the atonement of Jesus Christ.
18. Write a defense of the bodily resurrection of Jesus Christ.
19. Write a first-century newspaper article reporting the Resurrection of Jesus Christ.
20. Write a prayer of praise for the work of Jesus Christ.

Additional Activity:
The activity on the next page may be reproduced as a student worksheet.

Additional Activity, Answer Key

THE FATHER	THE SON	THE SPIRIT
Ephesians 1:3–5	Ephesians 1:7–11	Ephesians 1:13–14
Ephesians 1:17	Ephesians 1:20–23	Ephesians 5:18
Ephesians 2:4	Ephesians 2:13	Ephesians 6:17–18
Ephesians 2:6	Ephesians 2:13–18	
Ephesians 3:14	Ephesians 3:17	
Ephesians 4:6	Ephesians 4:8–10	
	Ephesians 5:2	

Additional verses may also be used.

THE APOSTLE PAUL AND THE DOCTRINE OF CHRIST

Using the Epistle to the Ephesians and a Bible concordance, list below the verses in that book that mention each member of the Godhead. Using the information you have gained from making this list, write a one-page report about what Paul was inspired to write concerning the Lord Jesus Christ in the Ephesian letter. Assume you have no other resources available to you to prepare this report. Use only the information revealed by God in the Epistle to the Ephesian church.

THE FATHER	THE SON	THE SPIRIT
_____	_____	_____
_____	_____	_____
_____	_____	_____
_____	_____	_____
_____	_____	_____
_____	_____	_____
_____	_____	_____
_____	_____	_____
_____	_____	_____
_____	_____	_____
_____	_____	_____

Materials Needed for LIFEPAC

Required:

Suggested:
Wall maps of the ancient Near East and the Land of Israel
Wall maps of modern Europe
King James Version of the Bible
Bible atlas
Bible handbook
Bible dictionary
Bible encyclopedia
Wood, Leon. *A Survey of Israel's History*. Grand Rapids, MI: Zondervan Publishing House, 1970.

Extended Writing Assignment

The student is to select one of the Old Testament periods listed on page 15 of this LIFEPAC. Using additional sources, the student is to develop a time line that portrays the major events of the period selected. Sources and dates are to be listed on the chart. Check for neatness and correct spacing of dates. If the student does an especially good job, the chart may be displayed in the classroom.

Additional Learning Activities

Section I The Abrahamic Covenant

1. Discuss the faith God required of Abraham. He was told to go to a distant land and was told he would have a son even though he was advanced in years. Consider, with the students, if believers today would follow the Lord in the same way.
2. By using a wall map or by making the classroom into a map of the Land of Israel, walk through the early events in Israel's history. Include Abraham's journey, the sojourn in Egypt, and the return under Moses to the land.
3. Allow a group of students to produce a skit that will portray any of the events in Abraham's life that relate to the promises of God. Have the students write a script, cast the skit, and produce it for the class.
4. Have a group of students make posters that explain the various covenants God made with His Old Testament people. Include the Abrahamic, Palestinian, Davidic, and New Covenants.
5. Make a wall-size time line that will show the important and major events in Israel's history from the time of Abraham to the time of Christ.
6. Make a chart that will show the kings of united Israel, Israel, and Judah from the time of Saul to the fall of the Southern Kingdom. Include the dates these kings reigned over God's people.
7. Read the book *The Source* by James A. Michener and prepare an oral or written report on it.

Section II The Significance of the Hebrew Nation

1. Discuss God's future for Israel. Question if the Old Testament promises will yet be realized in the nation of Israel or if the church has become the recipient of these promises. Discuss also whether the modern-day return of the Jews to Israel is an act of God or of man.

2. Discuss how the Jews have survived throughout the current era. Investigate the persecutions leveled against these people, especially during World War II.
3. Have a group of students make a report to the class on modern-day Reform, Conservative, and Orthodox Judaism. The students may wish to visit synagogues or speak with Jewish leaders or rabbis to further their investigations of these religions.
4. Have a group of students divide into two teams and debate and discuss the modern state of Israel. Have them consider the plight of the Palestinians and whether Israel should allow them to have a homeland within their borders.
5. Have a group of students debate the Jewish issue of anti Semitism. Is this attitude on the rise? Are the Jews really world conspirators? Should we fear the Jews as a people? Have the students consider what the Christian's attitude should be toward the Jews.
6. Using a concordance, find the New Testament reference to the Jews. Write a report on how the Jew is viewed by the New Testament writers.
7. Prepare and deliver to the class a dramatic reading or an oral report on Stephen's message in Acts chapter 7. Write an introduction that will relate the significance of this passage of Scripture.
8. Read a book on Adolf Hitler or World War II. Prepare an oral or written report on your findings.

Section III The Archaeological Discoveries
1. Discuss the important work that is accomplished by those who search for biblical documents. Explain how their discoveries help us to determine the original text of God's Word.
2. Discuss the ways in which all of the archaeological discoveries have validated the true record of the Bible. Explain the value of archaeological discoveries to the church today.
3. Invite a pastor or teacher who is well-read in the area of archaeology to come to the classroom and speak to the students.
4. In many parts of the country, archaeological digs are currently being undertaken in ancient Indian areas. If there is a dig currently in operation near your school, have a group of students visit the site and speak with the people involved. Contact your local college or university for additional information.
5. Have a group of students make a display using photocopies of various ancient manuscript discoveries. These can be found in most college and university libraries.
6. Have a group of students make plaster models of the various discoveries mentioned in this LIFEPAC.
7. Make a wall map that shows the locations of the various manuscript discoveries mentioned in this LIFEPAC.
8. Make a wall map of the various archaeological findings mentioned in this LIFEPAC.
9. Using additional sources, make a research report on the Dead Sea Scrolls.

Additional Activity
The activity on the next page may be reproduced as a student worksheet.

Additional Activity, Answer Key
1. Abrahamic Covenant
2. sojourn in Egypt
3. Exodus
4. Israel divided
5. Israel destroyed
6. Judah taken captive
7. Esther marries Xerxes
8. Alexander the Great ends Persian Empire
9. Seleucids gain control of the Land of Israel
10. Pompey takes Jerusalem
11. Romans destroy Jerusalem
12. Rome converts to Christianity
13. Spanish Inquisition
14. Adolf Hitler becomes Chancellor of Germany
15. United Nations' partition of the Land of Israel
16. Modern state of Israel founded
17. Arab hostility against Israel
18. the Six-Day War
19. war between Israel and Egypt
20. peace treaty signed between Israel and Egypt

THE HISTORY OF THE NATION OF ISRAEL

Many important dates and events have been mentioned in the LIFEPAC in relationship to Israel and the history of the Jews. Twenty dates are listed. Some of the events that occurred on these dates have been referred to in this study and others have not. Using additional sources, such as a Bible dictionary or encyclopedia, complete the chart below. Write the event that occurred in the year listed on the corresponding line.

1. 2100 B.C. _____

2. 1870 B.C. _____

3. 1440 B.C. _____

4. 930 B.C. _____

5. 722 B.C. _____

6. 587 B.C. _____

7. 478 B.C. _____

8. 333 B.C. _____

9. 199 B.C. _____

10. 63 B.C. _____

11. A.D. 70 _____

12. A.D. 313 _____

13. 1492 (Hint: Spain) _____

14. 1933 _____

15. 1947 _____

16. 1948 _____

17. 1953-56 _____

18. 1967 _____

19. 1976 _____

20. 1979 _____

Materials Needed for LIFEPAC
Required:

Suggested:
King James Version of the Bible
Other versions of the Bible if available and permitted
Bible handbook
Bible encyclopedia

Extended Writing Assignment

The student is to write a 500-word research paper using sources other than the LIFEPAC. The student is to select two Old Testament books and two New Testament books and prove their inspiration and authenticity. Both internal and external evidences are to be cited. A logical outline that follows a logical pattern is to be submitted for the Teacher check on page 30 of the LIFEPAC. The final draft is to be submitted for the Teacher check on page 32 of the LIFEPAC. Check for correct spelling, grammar, and paragraph and sentence structure.

Additional Learning Activities
  Section I The Doctrine of the Bible
1. Discuss the doctrines that relate to bibliology. Emphasize that God has delivered to us His perfect Word. Relate these doctrines to the idea that if God has done so much to deliver to us His Word, should we not study and live His Word?
2. Assign to each student in the class at least one book of the Bible. Have the students find at least one verse in their assigned book that attests to divine communication or inspiration. Have the students share their findings with their classmates.
3. Allow a group of students to debate and discuss the inspiration of the Bible. Divide the group into two teams. Have each team argue one position and then switch to the other position.
4. Allow a group of students to debate and discuss the revelation of God's truth. Is God still revealing Himself today? Is the canon complete? Are all the books of the Bible inspired?
5. Using the doctrines studied in Section I, have a group of students make various wall posters that illustrate these doctrines. Have the students incorporate Scripture into their illustrations.
6. Using additional sources, write a paper on one of the doctrines studied in this section of the LIFEPAC.
7. Make a chart or poster that illustrates the various ways in which God revealed Himself to man in the Old Testament.

  Section II The Formation of the Bible
1. Discuss the development of writing. Give examples of pictographs, idiographs, and phonograms. The students may even make up their own alphabets following these ancient forms.
2. Discuss what it would be like if we did not have written revelation from God. Explore the lack of confidence we would have without God's Word to stand upon as divine truth.
3. Have a group of students construct a time line that shows the formation of the Old Testament books.
4. Have a group of students make a chart that shows the theme of each of the New Testament books. Arrange the chart in chronological order and indicate date and author along with the recipient.

5. Allow a group of students to discuss the chronological order of the New Testament books. Have the group seek to determine if the New Testament should be kept in its present order or rearranged to its chronological order.

6. Make a chart that identifies the writers of the books of the Old Testament. Make the chart follow the Hebrew canon order of books.

7. Write a paper, using additional sources, on the Talmud. Identify its content, scope, and purpose.

8. Make a chart that identifies the theme of each of the latter Prophets and their writings.

Section III The Recognition of the Scriptures

1. Discuss what canonicity is. Emphasize that it is man's recognition of the Word of God and not merely man approving certain books and rejecting others.

2. A game may be played with the entire class by using the books of the Bible, the Pseudepigrapha, and the Apocrypha. Call out the title of one of these books and have individual students identify to which classification it belongs.

3. Have a spelling-and-definition bee using the vocabulary words introduced in this LIFEPAC.

4. Have a group of students collect copies of apocryphal books. Have the students discuss why the book is not to be considered part of the canon. Internal evidences should be listed by the group.

5. Have a group of students make a chart or wall poster that identifies the church fathers, apologists, and early theologians who contributed to the canonization of the New Testament.

6. Using additional sources, make a list of books that were considered but rejected as part of the New Testament canon.

7. Using additional sources, write a paper that explains the activities of one of the church councils listed in the LIFEPAC.

Additional Activity

The activity on the next page may be reproduced as a student worksheet.

Additional Activity, Answer Key

1. James
2. Mark
3. Matthew
4. 1 Thessalonians
5. 2 Thessalonians
6. Galatians
7. 1 Corinthians
8. 2 Corinthians
9. Romans
10. Ephesians
11. Colossians
12. Philemon
13. Philippians
14. Luke
15. Acts
16. 1 Timothy
17. Titus
18. 1 Peter
19. 2 Peter
20. 2 Timothy
21. Hebrews
22. Jude
23. 1 John
24. 2 John
25. 3 John
26. John
27. Revelation

THE CHRONOLOGICAL ORDER OF THE NEW TESTAMENT

You have studied the chronological order of the New Testament in this LIFEPAC. Now see if you can arrange the books of the New Testament into that order without the aid of additional sources. In the column on the left are listed the books of the New Testament as they appear in the King James Version of the Bible. List the chronological order in the center column, and write any corrections in the column on the right when you check your paper.

NEW TESTAMENT BOOKS	CHRONOLOGICAL ORDER	CORRECTIONS
1. Matthew	_____	_____
2. Mark	_____	_____
3. Luke	_____	_____
4. John	_____	_____
5. Acts	_____	_____
6. Romans	_____	_____
7. 1 Corinthians	_____	_____
8. 2 Corinthians	_____	_____
9. Galatians	_____	_____
10. Ephesians	_____	_____
11. Philippians	_____	_____
12. Colossians	_____	_____
13. 1 Thessalonians	_____	_____
14. 2 Thessalonians	_____	_____
14. 1 Timothy	_____	_____
15. 2 Timothy	_____	_____
16. Titus	_____	_____
17. Philemon	_____	_____
18. Hebrews	_____	_____
19. James	_____	_____
20. 1 Peter	_____	_____
21. 2 Peter	_____	_____
22. 1 John	_____	_____
23. 2 John	_____	_____
24. 3 John	_____	_____
25. Jude	_____	_____
26. Revelation	_____	_____

Materials Needed for LIFEPAC
> Required:

> Suggested:
> The Holy Bible, King James Version
> Shedd, Charlie W. *Letters to Karen*. Old
> Tappan, NJ: Fleming H. Revell Company,
> 1966.
> Shedd, Charlie W. *Letters to Philip*. Old
> Tappan, NJ: Fleming H. Revell Company,
> 1968.
> Hartley, Fred. *Update*. Grand Rapids, MI:
> Zondervan Publishing House, 1978.
> Hoffman, Sharon. *The Today Girl*. Old
> Tappan, NJ: Fleming H. Revell Company,
> 1975.
> Stafford, Tim. *A Love Story: Questions and
> Answers on Sex*. Grand Rapids: Zondervan
> Publishing House, 1978.

Extended Writing Assignment

The student is to first prepare questions to ask during an interview of a classmate. The interview should center on the attitudes concerning friendships. The student is to write a three- to four-page paper on the results of the interview. The student's own opinion regarding the other student's attitude toward friendship should be included in the final report. Check for a logical structure in the questions and the final paper, correct spelling and grammar, and advanced sentence structure.

Additional Learning Activities
Section I Friendship
1. Using David and Jonathan as an illustration, discuss the nature of true friendship. What is required in a friend and what is required of you by a friend? Use the verses mentioned in this section as additional references.
2. Discuss the responsibility of friendship. Consider the value of true friendship as opposed to being used by someone. Discuss whether or not all who may befriend you do so for the right reasons.
3. Have a group of students use role-playing, displaying various situations involving friends and those who call themselves friends but are not. You may have one student be in adversity and have the others react to him.
4. Have a group of students debate or discuss whether or not a Christian really needs friends. Have certain students argue that a believer does not need friends and then have the students reverse positions on the question.
5. Make a list of the friends you have. By each name write both how they are a friend to you and how you are a friend to them. Consider if there are any relationships you have that need to be improved.
6. Write a brief report on the nature of the friendship between David and Jonathan. Use Scripture references.

Section II Dating

1. Discuss the various activities in which Christian young men and women can engage when dating. Consider all types of activities and discuss which ones would best build positive values in the relationships.
2. Discuss the danger of merely Christianizing the secular practice of dating. Do believers also do this in other areas of life? Is this really doing all things as unto the Lord?
3. Have a group of students present a skit to the class in which a boy asks a girl for a date and then goes to her home to meet her parents. You may have this skit presented twice; one time it can be done incorrectly and the other time correctly.
4. Have a group of students present a panel discussion that will consider the question of whether or not Christians should date non-Christians. Have the class ask questions at the end of the discussion.
5. Write a paper on what you would consider an ideal dating situation for two Christian young people.
6. Interview your parents and find out what type of dating situations they were involved in as young people. Ask if their dating habits were what they would want for you. Write a brief report on your findings.

Section III Marriage

1. Discuss the customs regarding marriage in different cultures.
2. Discuss the rising divorce rate in our society. Compare this situation to what God has said about marriage in the Bible. What can be done about this American tragedy?
3. Have a group of students discuss and debate what is meant by the Scriptures which state that the husband is the head of the wife. Is this principle still true or was it a cultural rule applied only to Paul's day?
4. Have the students gather statistics on marriage and divorce in your community. Then, have them compare these to national norms to determine whether or not your community is close to one side or the other of the national average.
5. Write a brief report on what you think would be the ideal marriage. Compare your ideas on this subject to what the Bible says about marriage.
6. Write a paper in which you consider if it would ever be right for one partner in marriage to leave his/her spouse. Consider the difference between separation and divorce. Could one be biblical and not the other? Use Scripture to support your conclusions.

Additional Activity

The activity on the next page may be reproduced as a student worksheet.

Additional Activity, Answer Key

Any answers taken from Proverbs 31:10–31 will satisfy the requirements of this assignment.

THE VIRTUOUS WOMAN

In Proverbs 31:10–31, the Scriptures record a description of the godly woman. Study that passage of God's Word; on the lines below, make a list of her virtues, character, and activities.

1. _____
2. _____
3. _____
4. _____
5. _____
6. _____
7. _____
8. _____
9. _____
10. _____
11. _____
12. _____
13. _____
14. _____
15. _____
16. _____
17. _____
18. _____
19. _____
20. _____

Materials Needed for LIFEPAC

Required:

Suggested:
Wall map of the ancient Near East during the tenth century B.C.
King James Version of the Bible
Bible handbook
Bible atlas
Bible concordance
Bible dictionary
Bible encyclopedia
Wood, Leon. *A Survey of Israel's History*. Grand Rapids, MI: Zondervan Publishing House, 1970.

Extended Writing Assignment

The student is to write a two- to three-page paper on how Christians today attempt to find happiness apart from the grace of God. Examples and illustrations of a search for happiness in temporal things should be included in the report. The student should develop and follow a logical outline. Check for correct spelling, grammar, and sentence structure.

Additional Learning Activities

Section I Solomon's Succession

1. Discuss the unique position that Solomon enjoyed upon receiving the throne from David. Parallel this to the end of Solomon's reign when the nation was divided. Emphasis can be placed upon our responsibility to properly use the blessings we have. Have students give modern-day examples of similar situations.

2. Write an essay in which you answer the following: David advised Solomon on how to live for God. What advice does the New Testament give Christians on how to live for Christ? Use at least two New Testament passages in your answer.

3. Have a group of students make an illustrated time line of the reign of Solomon. Additional sources should be used and the completed project can be displayed in the classroom.

4. Make a chart comparing wisdom without God and wisdom with Him.

Section II Solomon's Prosperity

1. Take an interactive tour of Solomon's Temple at **www.3dbibleproject.com**.

2. Have a group of students make a model of the Temple that Solomon built as the house of the Lord.

3. Make a model of Solomon's throne for display in the classroom.

4. Discuss Solomon's search for happiness. Consider how his activities could have been used to bring glory to God rather than condemnation to Solomon. Stress that sometimes the mental attitude behind the activity is what separates it from being sin or a legitimate activity.

5. Discuss the process of distraction. Consider how Solomon was distracted from his spiritual responsibility and parallel that to the ways in which the Christian can fall away from the Lord today.

6. Discuss what it would have taken for Solomon to end his frantic search for happiness and return to the Lord's ways. Consider the graciousness of God in forgiving his people and their sins. Ask if there was ever a time when it was too late for Solomon to repent.

7. Have a group of students make posters of the various areas of Solomon's search for happiness. Include how these things can be either sin or used to bring glory to God.
8. Allow a class discussion of the various areas of human philosophy that were embraced by Solomon, particularly *hedonism*. Have some of the students support these ways of thinking and other students argue against them, using Scripture to show the right way.
9. Imagine that you are the editor of a Jerusalem newspaper. Write an editorial with a constructive criticism of Solomon and his fall into pride and idolatry. What would you have to say if he was your king?
10. Have a spelling-and-definition bee using the vocabulary words introduced in this LIFEPAC.

Section III Solomon's Reflections
1. Read Ecclesiastes and make a list of the verses that include the phrase "under the sun." List the areas to which Solomon ascribed that phrase.
2. Have a group of students present a group oral reading of the last chapters of Ecclesiastes, beginning in Ecclesiastes 9:13. Have the students divide the section and present the reading to the class.
3. Have a group of students make a large chart for display in the classroom that illustrates the outline of the book of Ecclesiastes.
4. Choose one or two verses from Proverbs. Create a poster reflecting the proverb or proverbs.
5. Research wise sayings or proverbs attributed to Benjamin Franklin. An example would be, "Write injuries in dust, benefits in marble." Write a paper in which you explore two or three of Franklin's sayings. Compare and contrast them with some of Solomon's wise sayings.
6. Using a wall map, show the limits of Solomon's kingdom and the areas that came under attack and fell into rebellion and eventual division as a result of Solomon's sin.
7. Discuss how divine rebuke and discipline is a mark of our membership in God's family. Consider how God disciplines out of His loving concern for His children. Ask what our reaction should be when we are rebuked.
8. Using a thesaurus, find at least one synonym and one antonym for each vocabulary word introduced in this LIFEPAC.
9. Write a brief report that describes the duty of man as eventually discovered by Solomon.

Additional Activity
The activity on the next page may be reproduced as a student worksheet.

Additional Activity, Answer Key
Any response is acceptable as long as it reasonably fits with the topic and the situation.

SOLOMON'S SPLENDOR

In this LIFEPAC you have studied how Solomon had wisdom, wealth, power, and position. Each of these, however, contributed to his downfall. Did they have to? On the lines below write a brief description of how these assets could have been used in the right manner and how they could have brought glory to God and the people over whom Solomon ruled.

WISDOM   _____

           _____

           _____

           _____

           _____

WEALTH   _____

           _____

           _____

           _____

           _____

POWER   _____

           _____

           _____

           _____

           _____

POSITION   _____

           _____

           _____

           _____

           _____

Materials Needed for LIFEPAC
Required:

Suggested:
King James Version of the Bible
Other versions of the Bible as available
and permitted
Bible handbook
Bible concordance
Bible dictionary
Morris, H. M. and M. Clark. *The Bible Has Answers*. San Diego: Creation-Life Company, 1976.
Torrey, R. A. *Difficulties in the Bible*. Chicago: Moody Press, 1907.

Extended Writing Assignment
None

Additional Learning Activities
Section I Questions About the Integrity of the Bible
1. Present and discuss one or more of the Moody science films.
2. Discuss what basis our faith would have if we rejected the authenticity of the Bible. Ask where truth for living would come from if we did not believe the Word of God.
3. Have a group of students use role-playing to act the parts of an atheist, an infidel, a skeptic, an agnostic, a critic, and an inquirer. Have each student present his viewpoint within his role.
4. Have a debate between two groups of students, with one group supporting a false view of the Bible and the other supporting the proper Christian view of the Scriptures. Have the teams switch positions for the second round of the debate.
5. Study commentaries and other books to find solutions to an apparent mistake in the Bible that is not mentioned in this LIFEPAC.
6. Read a book on science and the Bible recommended by your teacher, and give an oral report on it to the class.

Section II Questions about the Doctrines of the Bible
1. Discuss illustrations of the Trinity such as: three leaf clover; the three states of H_2O; man's body, soul, and spirit; sunshine's heat, light, and radiation; the three parts of an egg or an apple and a triangle. Explain their limitations.
2. Discuss how everything that happens can glorify God, especially evil and calamities.
3. Have students use role-playing as advocates of Christianity, Islam, Judaism, Mormonism, Jehovah's Witnesses, and any other religion with which a student is familiar. Debate the superiority of each.
4. Have a group of students search the Scriptures and determine what composes the essence of God. Have the students make a chart of the attributes of God, listing Scripture references. Display the chart in the classroom.
5. Ask a dozen Christians to prove that God exists, and tabulate the types of proof they use.
6. Take a man-on-the-street survey to discover people's opinions on who Jesus Christ is.
7. Take a man-on-the-street survey to discover people's opinions on heaven and hell, whether they exist, and who is going there.

Section III The Interpretation and Application of the Bible

1. Discuss what is traditional and what is biblical in our contemporary celebration of the nativity.
2. Discuss the nature of the unpardonable sin and the reasons for it.
3. Discuss the relationship of the two natures in the person of Jesus Christ.
4. Discuss what is cultural and what is biblical in worship today.
5. Discuss the differences and the similarities between God's requirements for Israel in the Old Testament and for Christians today, according to the New Testament.
6. Use role-playing to act out the various kinds of people around Jesus, such as the disciples, the multitudes, the Pharisees, the priests, and the Gentiles; and discuss their opinions about Him.
7. Have students share answers they have observed to prayer.
8. Write a short story on the memoirs of Cain, detailing the expansion of the human race.
9. Write an article for an imaginary newspaper in Noah's time, and report the changes brought by the Flood.
10. Read a book recommended by the teacher on the sightings of Noah's ark and give an oral report to the class.
11. Survey other students to learn how they know they are saved, and tabulate their bases for salvation.

Additional Activity

The activity on the next page may be reproduced as a student worksheet.

Additional Activity, Answer Key

First Day	Second Day	Third Day
light and darkness	heaven	land, vegetation, fruit, and herb trees
Fourth Day	**Fifth Day**	**Sixth Day**
sun, moon, stars	sea life, moving creatures, birds	living creatures, man and woman

OBSERVATIONS AND COMMENTS

The more complex fruit trees were created before the less complex sea creatures. Therefore, no process of evolution can be read into the creation account.

SCIENCE, CREATION, AND EVOLUTION

Many people attempt to make the humanistic process of evolution, and the theories it supports, compatible with the biblical account of Creation. Investigate Genesis 1:3–31 and see if this is possible. In the boxes below, list the events that occurred on each of the six days of the Creation account. Study the order of these things and consider if they are compatible with an evolutionary process. Write your findings on the lines below.

First Day	Second Day	Third Day
Fourth Day	Fifth Day	Sixth Day

OBSERVATIONS AND COMMENTS

_____

_____

_____

_____

_____

_____

_____

Materials Needed for LIFEPAC
Required:

Suggested:
King James Version of the Bible
Bible handbook
Bible atlas
Bible dictionary

Extended Writing Assignment

The student is to write a one-page report on how God has been faithful to him. This explanation should parallel and include the illustrations of God's faithfulness to David. Check for a logical outline and correct spelling, grammar, and sentence structure.

Additional Learning Activities

Section I The Uniqueness of the Bible

1. Discuss how God gave man His Word. Consider the many times the forces of darkness have tried to destroy the Bible but have not been able to do so.
2. Discuss the rules that were established by men regarding the canonization of the Bible. Emphasize that they were recognizing what God had inspired.
3. Have a group of students prepare a map of the Near East that shows the locations of the major archaeological discoveries that relate to the Scriptures. Identify as many discoveries as possible.
4. Have a group of students make a chart that displays the chronological order of the writing of the books of the Old and New Testaments.
5. Write a brief report on what Christianity would be like without the written revelation of God.
6. Make a list of all the known writers of the books of the Bible.

Section II The Book of Romans

1. Discuss how Roman culture and the Christian faith were bound to come into conflict. Contrast the Roman culture with the culture of the Greeks and the culture of the Jews.
2. A game may be played in which you read a verse from the book of Romans and the students must identify the chapter from which the verse came.
3. Have a group of students discuss why the beginning of Romans is different than the beginning of Paul's other Epistles.
4. Have a group of students do research and then make a number of posters that show outlines of the book of Romans other than the one given in this LIFEPAC.
5. Make a list and memorize the key verses from the book of Romans.
6. Make a map for display in the classroom that shows the physical features of the ancient city of Rome.

Section III The History of Israel

1. Discuss the contents of the Abrahamic Covenant. Consider the other covenants God has made with His people.
2. Discuss whether or not the modern state of Israel is a fulfillment of prophecy or merely a design of man.
3. Have a group of students make a time line of the history of the nation of Israel as described in the Old Testament.
4. Have a group of students discuss what God's plans are for His Old Testament people. Will God again deal with the Jews, or have His promises to them been given over to the church?

5. Make a list of nations, both ancient and modern, that have opposed or tried to destroy the Jews.
6. Make a chronological chart of the events that led to the 1979 peace accord between Israel, Egypt, and the United States.

Section IV The Revelation of God in the Bible
1. Discuss the divine and the human natures of Christ. Consider passages of Scripture that refer to these two natures.
2. Discuss what would have happened if the Lord Jesus Christ had not been raised from the dead. What would be the character of our faith had this great event not occurred?
3. Have a group of students make a time line of the earthly ministry of the Lord Jesus Christ.
4. Have a group of students make a poster that shows the reason and the results of the Lord's Ascension and Resurrection.
5. Make a list of at least ten passages of Scripture that directly refer to God's faithfulness and righteousness.
6. Outline 1 Corinthians 15, in which the apostle Paul explains the Resurrection of Christ.

Section V Principles for Christian Living
1. Discuss the ways in which Christian dating can be different than dating among unbelievers.
2. Discuss whether or not there is any difference between *friendship* and *fellowship*. Consider if unbelievers can have fellowship, or is this reserved only for the children of God?
3. Have a group of students consider the ways in which Solomon sought happiness. Have the students compare these avenues of temporal happiness to the ways in which men today seek happiness apart from God.
4. Have a group of students make a list of the things a believer in Christ must do if he is to mature. Have the group compare the way of life of the immature believer with that of the mature believer.
5. Write a report on whether or not the believer should date unbelievers. Use Scripture to support your answer.
6. Make a list of friends in the Bible. List those individuals who shared a common relationship and who are described as being friends.

Additional Activity
The activity on the next page may be reproduced as a student worksheet.

Additional Activity, answer key
Any reasonable response is acceptable.

THE GOAL OF CHRISTIAN LIVING

Throughout the Scriptures the child of God is encouraged to grow in the Lord. Using a concordance or topical Bible, find at least ten verses that encourage you to grow in the Lord. Write the location of these verses on the following lines.

1. _____

2. _____

3. _____

4. _____

5. _____

6. _____

7. _____

8. _____

9. _____

10. _____

Memorize as many of these verses as time permits.

ALTERNATE

TESTS

Reproducible Tests
for use with the Bible 1100
Teacher's Guide

Name _____

Answer *true* or *false* (each answer, 1 point).

1. _____ Job lost so many things—health, possessions, and family—that he even lost his faith in God.

2. _____ God has promised to supply all our wants and all our needs if we trust Him.

3. _____ Faithfulness is an attribute of God.

4. _____ The Shepherd Psalm is Psalm 24.

5. _____ A steward is not an owner, but simply a manager of his master's goods.

Match these verses with their references (each answer, 2 points).

6. _____ "But the fruit of the Spirit is love, joy, peace, long-suffering, gentleness, good-ness, faith [faithfulness] . . . against such there is no law."

    a. Hebrews 13:5

    b. 1 John 2:1

    c. Galatians 5:22 and 23

7. _____ "He hath said, I will never leave thee, nor forsake thee."

    d. 2 Timothy 2:13

8. _____ "If we believe not, yet he abideth faithful; he cannot deny himself."

    e. Romans 8:28

    f. Hebrews 1:7

9. _____ "And we know that all things work together for good to them that love God . . . ."

10. _____ "If any man sin, we have an advocate with the Father, Jesus Christ the righteous."

Complete these statements (each answer, 3 points).

11. The Bible records many _____ of men to the faithfulness of God.

12. "I will not fail thee nor _____ thee." (Joshua 1:5)

13. Psalm 23 is known as the _____ Psalm.

14. Some men make _____ of money, power, or pleasure.

15. When God says He will do this, if you will do that, that is a _____ promise.

16. "He that heareth my word, and believeth on him that sent me, hath

    _____ life." (John 5:24)

17. The Bible teaches that Christ was true a. _____ as

    well as true b. _____ .

18. The book of Hebrews compares the a. _____ of Christ,

    and the b. _____ of Aaron.

19. One of the duties of the high priest was to make _____
    to God for the people.

20. "So then faith cometh by hearing, and hearing by the word of _____

    _____ ." (Romans 10:17)

Complete these activities (each answer, 5 points).

21. What did God promise Joshua? _____

    _____

22. What verse in the book of Matthew gives a promise of the preservation

    of God's church? Give verse and reference. _____

    _____

Complete these activities (each answer, 3 points).

23. Give two reasons from 1 Kings 18:19-40 why Baal failed.

    a. _____

    b. _____

24. Write three things that the psalmist says the Good Shepherd does for us.

    a. _____

    b. _____

    c. _____

Match the following persons with their acts of faith (each answer, 2 points).

25. _____ left his country and people

26. _____ chose to suffer affliction with God's people

27. _____ 300 men victorious

28. _____ perished not

29. _____ found grace in the eyes of the Lord

a. Moses

b. Gideon

c. Noah

d. Abraham

e. Rahab

f. Samson

69 / 86

Date _____

Score _____

Bible 1102 Alternate Test

Name _____

Match these items (each answer, 2 points).

1. _____ Jesus   a. sanctification

2. _____ Holy Spirit   b. servant

3. _____ Adam   c. salvation

4. _____ Paul   d. betrayal

5. _____ Abraham   e. saved by faith

                              f. sin

Answer *true* or *false* (each answer, 1 point).

6. _____ The nature of condemnation is judgment.

7. _____ Justification brought righteousness and life.

8. _____ The carnal nature is basically disciplined.

9. _____ The result of sin is death.

10. _____ The law is evil.

Write the letter for the correct answer on each line (each answer, 2 points).

11. Sanctification is the means whereby saints are _____.

   a. justified   c. glorified
   b. preserved   d. redeemed

12. The Roman Empire included the land area around _____.

   a. Africa   c. the Mediterranean Sea
   b. Asia Minor   d. Europe

13. The Roman religious policy was _____.

   a. pantheism   c. indifference
   b. emperor worship   d. syncretism

14. When moving into a new area for the purpose of evangelizing, the apostles
     generally went first to a _____.

   a. home church   c. synagogue
   b. love feast   d. forum

15. Not included in the salutation to the Roman letter was the _____.

   a. greeting
   b. prayer of thanksgiving
   c. exhortation
   d. name of the sender and the addressee

68

Complete these statements (each answer, 3 points).

16. Paul probably wrote Romans during the winter of A.D. _____.

17. Paul wanted to commend _____ to the church at Rome.

18. The law provoked _____ and then became a means of condemnation.

19. *To make amends, reconcile,* or *to be at one with someone* is known as

_____ .

20. The Roman state religion was _____ .

Complete the following activities (each answer, 3 points).

21. List the first five Roman emperors.

    a. _____   d. _____

    b. _____   e. _____

    c. _____

22. Summarize the first eight chapters of Romans chapter by chapter.

    a. Romans 1:1-17 _____

    b. Romans 1:18 - 2:29 _____

    c. Romans chapter 3 _____

    d. Romans chapter 4 _____

    e. Romans chapter 5 _____

    f. Romans chapter 6 _____

    g. Romans chapter 7 _____

    h. Romans chapter 8 _____

23. From memory write the following Scripture verses.

    a. Romans 1:16 and 17 _____

    _____

    _____

    _____

    _____

b. Romans 3:23 _____

_____

c. Romans 6:23 _____

_____

d. Romans 5:1 _____

_____

e. Romans 5:8 _____

_____

f. Romans 6:11 _____

_____

g. Romans 8:1 _____

_____

Answer the following question (this answer, 5 points).

24. What was the error of the Judaizers, and how did Paul refute it?

_____

_____

_____

_____

_____

_____

_____

| 84 / |
| / 105 |

Date _____

Score _____

Name _____

Match these items (each answer, 2 points).

1. _____ imperial worship

2. _____ Paul's letter bearer

3. _____ peace

4. _____ government officials

5. _____ Priscilla and Aquila

6. _____ victory that overcomes the world

7. _____ second rank social class

8. _____ monotheism

9. _____ word of testimony

10. _____ remission of sin

a. fruit of justification

b. belief in one God

c. our faith

d. blood of the lamb

e. loyalty to the emperor

f. destroyer of faith

g. Phoebe

h. Paul's friend

i. God's ministers

j. equestrian

k. Peter's cousins

Answer *true* or *false* (each answer, 1 point).

11. _____ Everyone has sinned.

12. _____ We have been saved, are being saved, and will be saved.

13. _____ A factor in spiritual maturity is suffering.

14. _____ Vengeance belongs to man.

15. _____ Jesus came to destroy the Law.

Write the letter for the correct answer on each line (each answer, 2 points).

16. The symbol of our death and resurrection with Jesus is_____.

    a. circumcision
    b. baptism
    c. justification
    d. a, b, and c

17. In Romans 11, the Jewish nation is represented by the _____.

    a. roots
    b. wild olive branch
    c. branches broken off
    d. none of these

18. The victorious ones spoken of in the Revelation are called _____.

    a. justifiers
    b. trees of righteousness
    c. pillars
    d. overcomers

19. The wild olive branch in Romans chapter 11 is symbolic of _____.

    a. the Gentiles
    b. the Jewish nation as a whole
    c. the Jewish remnant
    d. the covenant promises

20. Jesus came as the _____ of the Law.

    a. sanctification
    b. judge
    c. fulfillment
    d. Savior

21. We cannot escape temptation by relying on _____.

    a. prayer
    b. the Christian's armor
    c. our human goodness
    d. God's Word

22. The human heart is _____.

    a. good
    b. free from guilt
    c. turned towards God
    d. deceitful and wicked

23. A covered walkway is called a _____.

    a. labyrinth
    b. intrigue
    c. promenade
    d. forum

24. The Jews had a zeal for God but lacked _____.

    a. strength
    b. knowledge
    c. awareness
    d. instruction

25. The gifts and offices of the _____ are to be used for the edification of the body.

    a. Holy Spirit
    b. Father
    c. Son
    d. none of these

Complete this activity (each answer, 3 points).

26. List five of the seven gifts Paul speaks of in Romans 12:6–8.

    a. _____

    b. _____

    c. _____

    d. _____

    e. _____

Complete this activity (each answer, 2 points).

27. Write the chapter number of Romans next to the description.

   a. _____ God's sovereignty

   b. _____ reckoning justification by baptism

   c. _____ Abraham

   d. _____ unity

   e. _____ universal sin and guilt

   f. _____ carnal nature versus the spiritual nature

   g. _____ scruples

   h. _____ justification

   i. _____ submission

   j. _____ grafting of the Gentiles

Write these verses (each verse, 5 points).

28. Write from memory Romans 10:9 and 10. _____

   _____

   _____

29. Write from memory Romans 10:13. _____

   _____

   _____

30. Write from memory Romans 8:32. _____

   _____

31. Write from memory Romans 10:17. _____

   _____

   _____

80 / 100

Date _____

Score _____

Bible 1104 Alternate Test

ALTERNATE LIFEPAC TEST   Name _____

Match these items (each answer, 2 points).

1. _____ doctrine   a. anointed one

2. _____ Docetics   b. divine attribute

3. _____ Christ   c. substitution

4. _____ Socinus   d. body not real

5. _____ Son of man   e. defense lawyer

6. _____ immutable   f. Biblical subject

7. _____ angel of the Lord   g. Jesus adopted

8. _____ atonement   h. propitiation

9. _____ advocate   i. ransom

10. _____ satisfaction   j. Shekinah glory

                                   k. used for Ezekiel

Write *true* or *false* (each answer, 1 point).

11. _____ Christians are sons of God in the same sense that Christ is.

12. _____ Jesus Christ surrendered some of His divine attributes when He
             became a man.

13. _____ The Chalcedonian Creed teaches Christ's *kenosis*.

14. _____ Many skeptics question the existence of Jesus as a historical
             person.

15. _____ Although Jesus was God, He had to eat, drink, and sleep while on earth.

16. _____ Jesus Christ is the visible person of the Godhead in the Old
             Testament.

17. _____ Jesus gave special privileges to some of His disciples.

18. _____ Jesus Christ achieved His greatest and most significant work in
             His death.

19. _____ Christ's ransom on the cross forces Satan to release captive
             souls.

20. _____ Barabbas illustrates redemption.

21. _____ Our resurrection bodies will resemble that of Jesus Christ.

22. _____ When the disciples first saw the resurrected Christ, they adopted the theory that He was a spirit.

23. _____ According to Hodge, the resurrection of Christ is partially authenticated as a historical fact.

24. _____ Christ is active in the Church, though He is in heaven.

25. _____ Our nation's ambassadors illustrate Christ's earthly ministry.

Write the letter for the correct answer on each line (each answer, 2 points).

26. Truths about Jesus Christ come from _____.

   a. the entire Old Testament   c. the four Gospels
   b. the entire New Testament   d. all of these

27. Many non-Christian religions view Jesus Christ as just another of the great biblical_____.

   a. prophets   c. kings
   b. priests   d. angels

28. The name of Jesus Christ that does not identify Him with His people is _____.

   a. Christ   c. Son of man
   b. Son of God   d. Savior

29. The deity of Jesus Christ is taught in _____.

   a. Isaiah 9:6   c. a and b
   b. John 1:1   d. neither a nor b

30. Jesus had _____ parents.

   a. no   c. no human and one divine
   b. one human and no divine   d. one human and one divine

31. While He was on earth, Jesus Christ was _____.

   a. omniscient   c. omnipresent
   b. omnipotent   d. a, b, and c

32. Jesus Christ is _____.

   a. still a man   c. both a and b
   b. a member of the Godhead   d. neither a nor b

33. The angel of the Lord is _____.

   a. the Son of God   c. the Redeemer
   b. God   d. a, b, and c

34. Jesus'_____ validated Him and His divine message.

    a. miracles   c. personality
    b. disciples   d. sincerity

35. Divorce illustrates man's need for _____.

    a. redemption   c. reconciliation
    b. satisfaction   d. atonement

36. That which demonstrates the completed work of the Cross is _____.

    a. Christ's Incarnation   c. Christ's present ministry
    b. Christ's Resurrection   d. our salvation

37. Jesus appeared to _____ people after His Resurrection.

    a. twelve   c. a few hundred
    b. seven thousand   d. over five hundred

Complete these statements (each answer, 3 points).

38. The Word of God in written form is _____.

39. That which cleanses from all sin is the_____of Christ.

40. The true view of the atonement interprets the death of Christ as a _____.

Complete this activity (this answer, 5 points).

41. Write from memory one of the following verses: Isaiah 9:6; Mark 10:45; Luke 2:52; John 1:1; I Timothy 2:5; or I Peter 1:18 and 19.

    _____

    _____

    _____

58 / 73

Date _____

Score _____

Name _____

Match these items (each answer, 2 points).

1. _____ first king of Persia

2. _____ Ptolemies

3. _____ sacrificed swine in Temple

4. _____ Hirrians

5. _____ Christian voice for Jews in Germany

6. _____ people of the scrolls

7. _____ carved on a mountain

8. _____ prophet and judge of Israel

9. _____ Bar Kochba revolt

10. _____ Seleucids

11. _____ Church of the Nativity

12. _____ Moslem religion

13. _____ reveals Canaanite evil

14. _____ anti-Roman Jews

15. _____ ancient market place

16. _____ Saul and David

17. _____ Code of Hammurabi

18. _____ ten lost tribes of Israel

19. _____ temple of Diana

20. _____ binding and solemn agreement

a. Babylonian way of life

b. Horites

c. Essenes

d. Ephesus

e. Emperor Hadrian

f. Behistun Inscription

g. Cyrus

h. Ras Shamra tablets

i. Jerusalem

j. Antiochus Epiphanes

k. agora

l. covenant

m. Lessing

n. Samuel

o. Egypt

p. Zealots

q. Syria

r. Islam

s. Northern Kingdom

t. United Kingdom

u. Greece

Write *true* or *false* (each answer, 1 point).

21. _____ The first king of Israel's Southern Kingdom was Omri.

22. _____ The Greek translation of the Old Testament is the Septuagint.

23. _____ The first North American Jewish settlement was in New Amsterdam.

77

24. _____ The Rosetta Stone describes the exploits of Darius.

25. _____ The center of Diana worship was the city of Corinth.

Complete these statements (each answer, 3 points).

26. The discovery that reveals the conditions in Palestine prior to Joshua's conquest of the land is the _____ .

27. The discovery that dates to the time of the wars between Mesha and Omri is the _____ .

28. Abraham's name means *the* _____ .

29. The woman God used as the protectoress of the Jews was _____ .

30. The chancellor of the German Reich was _____ .

31. The man who wanted a home for the Jews in France was _____ .

32. Ruth was from _____ .

33. The first king of the Northern Kingdom was _____ .

34. Abraham's son of promise was _____ .

35. Constantine moved the capital of _____ to Byzantium.

Write the events that occurred on the following dates (each answer, 3 points).

36. June 5 to June 11, 1967 _____

37. 722 B.C. _____

38. A.D. 313 _____

39. 1939 to 1945 _____

40. A.D. 70 _____

72 / 90

Date _____

Score _____

Match these items (each answer, 2 points).

1. _____ Revelation
2. _____ Deuteronomy
3. _____ kanon
4. _____ apostolos
5. _____ canonicity
6. _____ *Kethubim*
7. _____ rainbow
8. _____ exegesis
9. _____ infallible
10. _____ James I

a. Greek term meaning: one who is sent forth

b. a scientific process by which writings are adjudged to be Holy Scripture

c. symbol of God's everlasting covenant with all creatures

d. absolutely trustworthy; unfailing in effectiveness, certain

e. God's disclosure of himself and his will to his creatures

f. "second giving of the law," fifth book of Moses

g. Greek name of a reed that was used as a measuring stick

h. king who authorized an English version of the Bible

i. critical explanation or interpretation of a text

j. Hebrew term for the Writings

Write *true* or *false* (each answer, 1 point).

11. _____ Authors of Holy Scripture never realized they were writing the Word of God.

12. _____ God, Himself, is the single, primary author of the Bible.

13. _____ Authenticity and authorship of the Pentateuch has always been controversial.

14. _____ One cannot decide the canonicity of O.T. books apart from N.T. testimony.

15. _____ Peter used a nautical analogy depicting divine inspiration as wind driving a ship.

16. _____ Theophilus was the author of the Gospel of Luke and of the Acts of the Apostles.

17. _____ All the known authors of the New Testament were either apostles or their immediate delegates.

18. _____ New Testament authors rarely, if ever, refer to the five books of Moses, the Law.

19. _____ Any writing accepted into the canon had to be originally accepted as God's Word and subsequently confirmed as such.

20. _____ Verbal, plenary inspiration characterizes the Bible, and only the Bible.

Write the letter for the correct answer on each blank (each answer, 2 points).

21. God's primary method of revealing himself and his will today is _____ .
    a. visions
    b. the Bible
    c. signs and wonders
    d. christophanies

22. The Hebrew title of the books of Moses (the Book of the Law) is _____ .
    a. the Torah
    b. the Writings
    c. the Apocrypha
    d. the Amarna Letters

23. Mark relied on _____ eyewitness account to write his Gospel.
    a. John's
    b. James'
    c. Peter's
    d. Matthew's

24. The _____ is a group of writings regarded as non-canonical and considered fake or counterfeit writings.
    a. Apocrypha
    c. Pentateuch
    b. Pseudepigrapha
    d. Septuagint

25. Apologist _____ quoted extensively from Scripture in his defense of Christianity.
    a. Clement of Rome
    c. Irenaeus
    b. Apollos
    d. Eusebius

Complete these activities (each answer, 3 points).

26. Specific revelation, the Word of God, is presented in what two forms?

    a. _____ and b. _____

27. A _____ occurred when God appeared in the form of an angel or a man.

28. Submission to God's authority places one in the position of maximum

    a._____ and b. _____ .

29. From Creation, the story of God's interaction with people spans at least _____ years before Moses wrote the Torah.

30. At Sinai, with the publication of the Torah, the children of Israel were led and equipped by God to move beyond tribalism and become a holy _____ .

31. Name the subsets of writings contained in the Latter Prophets:

    a. _____

    b. _____

32. In 280 B.C., a new translation of the Hebrew Old Testament by 72 Hebrew-Greek scholars in Alexandria, Egypt, called the _____ , ensured that upcoming generations of Greek-speaking Jews would be able to read and understand the Scriptures.

33. The Greek word translated inspired in 2 Timothy 3:16 literally means _____ .

34. The N.T. book for which authorship is still being debated is _____ .

35. Which branches of the Christian church included the Apocrypha in the canon of Holy Scripture?
    a. _____ and b. _____ .

Complete these Bible verses from memory (each answer, 2 points)

36. "For this cause also _____ we God without ceasing, because, when ye received the _____ of God which ye heard of us, ye received it not as the word of men, but as it is in truth, the word of _____ , which effectually worketh also in you that _____ ." (1 Thessalonians 2:13).

37. "When a prophet _____ in the name of the LORD, if the thing _____ not, nor come to pass, that is the thing which the LORD hath _____ spoken, but the prophet hath spoken it presumptuously: thou shalt not be _____ of him" (Deuteronomy 18:22).

38. "All Scripture is _____ by God and _____ for teaching, for reproof, for correction, for training in _____ " (2 Timothy 3:16).

39. "And I will put _____ between thee [serpent] and the woman, and between thy seed and her _____ ; it shall bruise thy _____ , and thou shalt bruise his heel." (Genesis 3:15).

88 / 110

Date _____

Score _____

Name _____

Match these items (each answer, 2 points).

1. _____ condone

2. _____ figurative

3. _____ cherish

4. _____ prejudice

5. _____ incompatible

6. _____ cleave

7. _____ virtuous

8. _____ thwart

9. _____ culture

10. _____ adversity

a. hardship

b. an established purpose

c. treat with tenderness

d. firmly adhere to

e. to allow

f. pattern of collective behavior

g. not literal

h. lack of harmony

i. to frustrate

j. premature judgment

k. moral excellence

Write *true* or *false* (each answer, 1 point).

11. _____ For a Christian, friendship is not necessary in life.

12. _____ Our relationship with the Lord can teach us about our relationship to our friends.

13. _____ All we need to do to make dating holy is Christianize the secular practice of dating.

14. _____ Isolation is required in dating situations.

15. _____ Dating can meet social and spiritual needs.

16. _____ Christian dating prepares the believer for Christian marriage.

17. _____ When dating an unbeliever, the Christian should adopt the principles of the unbeliever so as not to offend them.

18. _____ Dating includes prearranged agreement.

19. _____ In our society, marriage is in serious trouble.

20. _____ The marriage relationship is a result of fallen man's passion and lust.

Complete these statements (each answer, 3 points).

21. Dating is a _____ engagement.

22. Dating must have specific _____.

23. God's decreed principle for marriage is to a. _____

    and b._____.

24. Marriage is a picture of a._____ relationship to

    the b. _____.

25. Marriage is bound by_____.

26. Marriage and the home compose the smallest _____ unit.

27. The teaching of Paul in 1 Corinthians 7:13 declares that the unbelieving

    husband is _____ by the wife.

28. In marriage, leadership belongs to the _____.

29. Proverbs chapter 31 teaches about the _____ woman.

30. First Peter 3:1 tells the wife to be in _____ to her own
    husband.

31. Ephesians 5:23 states that the husband is the _____ of the
    wife.

Complete these activities (each answer, 3 points).

32. List the two areas of the possibilities for friendship.

    a. _____   b. _____

33. List two personal responsibilities for friendship.

    a. _____   b. _____

34. List four blessings God invoked upon Adam and the woman.

    a. _____   c. _____

    b. _____   d. _____

35. List three characteristics of a friend mentioned in Proverbs.

   a. _____   c. _____

   b. _____

```
┌─────────┐
│ 82 ╱    │
│   ╱ 102 │
└─────────┘
```

Date _____

Score _____

Matching (each answer, 2 points).

1. _____ anoint
2. _____ consolidating
3. _____ thesis
4. _____ counterpoint
5. _____ accolades
6. _____ capricious
7. _____ conscripted
8. _____ beneficiary
9. _____ remnant
10. _____ competency
11. _____ deter
12. _____ diatribe

a. uniting; bringing together
b. a sacred ceremony in which oil is applied
c. main theme, subject, or argument of a paper
d. changeable
e. praises
f. small remaining part
g. forced into service
h. ability
i. person who receives benefits
j. a bitter attack or criticism
k. something which contrasts with another
l. to check or hinder

Absalom	Nathan	Rehoboam	high places
Adonijah	Jeroboam	Euphrates	Mount Moriah
David	Queen of Sheba	Gibeon	Tyre

Fill in the blanks using the words from the list above (each answer, 2 points).

13. The plan made by _____ to take over his father's kingdom was mimicked by his younger brother, Adonijah.

14. Abraham traveled to _____ to sacrifice his son, Isaac.

15. God appeared to Solomon in a dream at _____ after Israel's king had made sacrifices.

16. The prophet _____ warned Bathsheba of the plot to take over the throne promised to her son.

17. _____ was a port city on the Mediterranean.

18. God promised _____ that a member of his family would rule God's people forever.

19. Solomon made offerings to foreign gods at the _____ .

20. _____ tried to preserve his life by holding onto the horns of the altar.

21. The _____ traveled many miles to witness Solomon's wisdom.

22. _____ would rule over ten of the tribes of Israel following Solomon's death.

23. The _____ River was the northern boundary of Israel during the reign of Solomon.

24. _____ was Solomon's son and heir to the throne.

Bible 1108 Alternate Test

Sequencing: Number the following events in the correct order (each answer, 2 points).

25. _____ Rehoboam ruled over the tribes of Judah and Benjamin.

26. _____ David and Solomon ruled over Israel together.

27. _____ Solomon asked God for wisdom.

28. _____ Solomon worshipped foreign gods.

29. _____ Adonijah planned to become king after his father.

30. _____ Solomon built a palace for himself.

31. _____ David promised Bathsheba her son would be king after him.

32. _____ Solomon dedicated God's temple.

Write *true* or *false* (each answer, 1 point).

33. _____ Joab and Abiathar backed Solomon's claim to the throne.

34. _____ The title of Ecclesiastes can be translated to mean wisdom teacher.

35. _____ Most kings during the time of Solomon killed their rivals.

36. _____ Jesus filled God's promise to David of a ruler of David's family on the throne forever.

37. _____ God's glory filled the palace showing God's blessing on it.

38. _____ The temple Solomon built in Jerusalem would last a thousand years.

39. _____ Solomon heavily taxed his people.

40. _____ Solomon sealed his treaty with Egypt by presenting Pharaoh his royal throne.

41. _____ God showed his acceptance of the temple by having fire coming from heaven and consume the sacrifices.

42. _____ The phrase "vanity of vanities" is repeated over 50 times in the book of Ecclesiastes.

43. _____ Wisdom comes from knowing and following God's word.

44. _____ Apart from God, life is meaningless.

Multiple Choice: Circle the letter of the correct answer (each answer, 2 points).

45. Rehoboam would eventually rule _____ tribes of Israel.
    a. two   b. five   c. ten

46. Solomon reigned about _____ with King David.
    a. 2 months   b. 2 years   c. 6 months

47. Early in his reign, Solomon traveled to _____ to offer sacrifices.
    a. Jerusalem   b. Shiloh   c. Gibeon

48. _____ anointed kings who did not follow the natural order of kingly succession.
    a. priests   b. prophets   c. kings

49. The gods of Solomon's wives promoted _____ and child sacrifice.
    a. war   b. prostitution   c. harmony

50. Solomon's borders stretched from Egypt to the _____ River.

a. Nile   b. Tigris   c. Euphrates

51. Solomon asked God for _____ .

a. wisdom   b. wealth   c. power

52. _____ assisted Solomon in training sailors for Israel's fleet.

a. Pharaoh   b. King Hiram   c. King Nebuchadnezzar

53. Essay Questions: Choose one (this answer, 7 points).

a. Describe the temptations Solomon faced as Israel's king. How did they cause his relationship with God to deteriorate? Describe the temptations Christians face today. How can they cause their relationship with God to deteriorate?

b. What promises did God make to David and Solomon? How did God keep them?

79 / 99

Date _____

Score _____

Bible 1109 Alternate Test

Name _____

Match these items (each answer, 2 points).

1. _____ deduction   a. natural revelation

2. _____ induction   b. exaggeration

3. _____ secular   c. variation

4. _____ metaphor   d. gradual development

5. _____ hyperbole   e. exercises faith

6. _____ uniformitarianism   f. not religious

7. _____ science   g. violation of natural law

8. _____ mutation   h. exercises scholarship

9. _____ intervention   i. comparison

                               j. idolatry

Answer *true* or *false* (each answer, 1 point).

10. _____ Very little Bible criticism is constructive.

11. _____ A Christian with honest doubts should suspend his judgment.

12. _____ Matthew 27:9 credits Jeremiah with a quotation that resembles Zachariah 11:12 and 13 because a scribe copied the wrong name.

13. _____ In the Old Testament, God appeared only as an angel.

14. _____ The accounts of Jesus' beatitudes differ because they were given on two different occasions.

15. _____ Pleiades and Orion are two rivers mentioned in the Bible.

16. _____ Part truth is better than no truth.

17. _____ The Bible never attempts to prove God's existence.

18. _____ The analogy of a watchmaker illustrates the anthropological argument.

19. _____ The body's own healing process is a miracle.

Write the letter for the correct answer on each line (each answer, 2 points).

20. A skeptic is one who is _____.

    a. unbelieving   c. not knowing
    b. questioning   d. none of these

21. Natural phenomena are described from the human standpoint by _____.

    a. the Bible   c. archaeologists
    b. scientists   d. astronomers

22. All religions seek acceptance by _____.

    a. human merit   c. intuition
    b. sacrifice   d. prayer

23. According to Isaiah 45:7, God creates _____.

    a. sin   c. demons
    b. calamity   d. moral evil

24. The heathen are _____.

    a. not condemned by God
    b. excused by God
    c. more guilty than those who have rejected the gospel
    d. none of these

25. Heaven is the abode of _____.

    a. infants who die   c. departed Christians
    b. God   d. a, b, and c

26. Cain's wife may have been _____.

    a. his niece   c. his wife and his sister
    b. his sister   d. his aunt

27. Jesus possessed all knowledge _____.

    a. in his human nature c. known to man
    b. in his divine nature d. of evil

28. Assurance of salvation is *not* based upon _____.

    a. feelings
    b. the witness of the Holy Spirit
    c. God's promises
    d. faith

29. Answered prayer requires _____.

    a. obedience   c. faith
    b. patience   d. a, b, and c

30. God expects _____ to keep the Ten Commandments today.

    a. Jews   c. everyone
    b. Christians   d. no one

31. The Canaanites whom God commanded Israel to slaughter were _____.

    a. religious   c. persecutors of the Jews
    b. very moral   d. all killed

Complete these statements (each answer, 3 points).

32. The Bible contains more apparent contradictions involving _____ than any other category.

33. All men seem to have a desire to _____ someone or something.

34. The *Trinity* means *three* _____.

35. Jesus identified the unpardonable sin as _____.

Complete this activity (this answer, 5 points).

36. Write out 2 Timothy 3:16 and 17 from memory.

_____

_____

_____

_____

55 / 69

Date _____

Score _____

Name _____

Match these items (each answer, 2 points).

1. _____ didatic   a.   ever watchful

2. _____ remission   b.   without error

3. _____ omnipotent   c.   simple system of writing

4. _____ inerrant   d.   a critical analysis

5. _____ temporal   e.   used for the purpose of teaching

6. _____ insurgence   f.   to grant to another

7. _____ omniscient   g.   cancellation of a debt

8. _____ cleaving   h.   destruction of a people

9. _____ demotic   i.   widespread destruction

10. _____ holocaust   j.   a military uprising

11. _____ impute   k.   all powerful

12. _____ genocide   l.   all knowing

13. _____ omnipresent   m.   always present

14. _____ context   n.   related to time

15. _____ exegesis   o.   firmly adhearing to

     p.   within a specific setting

Answer *true* or *false* (each answer, 1 point).

16. _____ Prior to the Incarnation, God did not reveal Himself.

17. _____ Discipline, wisdom, and diligence are required for Bible study.

18. _____ The Megilloth includes the books of Job and Psalms.

19. _____ The Pseudepigrapha has no authenticity.

20. _____ The Roman Empire included many nations.

21. _____ Paul illustrated the body of Christ by referring to the human body.

22. _____ Abraham was the first Hebrew.

23. _____ The book of Romans was probably written from Ephesus.

24. _____ Judah was first ruled by Rehoboam.

25. _____ Bar Kochba was a Roman who fought against the Jews.

26. _____ Moses and Joshua were types of Christ.

27. _____ Psalm 23 refers to God's faithfulness.

28. _____ Jesus was part man and part God.

29. _____ Christ ascended prior to His Resurrection.

30. _____ Dating is prohibited in the Bible.

Complete these statements (each answer, 3 points).

31. David's closest friend was _____ .

32. Solomon eventually recognized that God brings every work into

    _____ .

33. The Scriptures are given by the _____ of God.

34. In 1947 a Bedouin goat herder discovered the _____ .

35. Some Romans believed that the _____ were gods.

36. In Romans Paul told of his plans to visit a. _____ and

    b. _____ .

37. God established a _____ with Abraham.

38. Every book of the Bible attests to God's _____ .

39. Paul taught that Christians were to be God's instruments of

    _____ .

40. The modern state of Israel was born on May 14, _____ .

Complete these activities (each answer, 3 points).

41. List three post-Apostolic ages of the Christian church.

    a. _____   c. _____

    b. _____

42. List four major archaeological discoveries that have enhanced the understanding of the Scriptures.

    a. _____   c. _____

    b. _____   d. _____

43. List the three kings of Israel who ruled a united kingdom.

    a. _____   c. _____

    b. _____

44. List three world leaders who worked for peace in the Middle East in 1979.

    a. _____   c. _____

    b. _____

94 / 117

Date _____

Score _____

ANSWER KEYS

Section One

1.1 a. vs. 24 "But my faithfulness and my mercy shall be with him."
b. vs. 33 "Nevertheless my loving-kindness will I not utterly take from him, nor suffer my faithfulness to fail."

1.2 d

1.3 a or h

1.4 h or a

1.5 i

1.6 e or j

1.7 j or e

1.8 f

1.9 g

1.10 b

1.11 c

1.12 Example:
an attitude of God implying loyalty, constancy, and freedom from arbitrariness or fickleness. Handy Dictionary of the Bible—Established by Merrill C. Tenny

1.13 that he would not fail him nor forsake him.

1.14 I will perform the oath which I swore unto Abraham thy father.

1.15 Behold, I am with thee, and will keep thee in all places whither thou goest, and will bring thee again into this land; for I will not leave thee, until I have done that which I have spoken to thee of.

1.16 I will never leave thee nor forsake thee.

1.17 Example:
God promised to be with His people and to do that which He has promised.

1.18 teacher check

1.19 teacher check

1.20 Examples:
a. Thanks to the Lord for his mercy
b. Thanks to the Lord for his work of creation
c. Thanks to the Lord for His deliverance of Israel
d. Thanks to the Lord for His provision for all flesh
e. Thanks to the God of Heaven

1.21 Any order:
a. the heavens
b. the earth above the waters
c. the great lights
d. the sun to rule by day
e. the moon, the stars to rule by night

1.22 Any order:
a. to him that smote Egypt in their firstborn
b. to him which divided the Red Sea into parts
c. to him which led his people through the wilderness
d. to him which smote great kings

1.23 Matthew 16:18 "The gates of hell shall not prevail against it" (the Church)

1.24 God's Word will accomplish His purpose.

1.25 Any order:
a. the universe
b. mankind
c. His chosen people, Israel
d. His called-out ones, the Church
e. His Word, our Bible

1.26 teacher check

1.27 teacher check

1.28 a. vs. 1
b. vs. 2, 3
c. vs. 4, 5
d. vs. 6

1.29 a. Example:
Jehovah Himself is the One to whom I belong and the One Who cares for me with all His omnipotence, ominscience, omnipresence, love, mercy, and grace.
b. Example:
He knows me personally: He sought me, found me, calls me by my name, meets all my needs, gives His life for me, and makes provision for me for eternity.
c. Example:
I am as a sheep, helpless, defenseless, open to the dangers of life, but He understands my condition and limitations and in love is all I need.

1.30 Example:
I have no needs unmet if the Lord is my shepherd.

1.31 b

1.32 f

1.33 e

1.34 g

1.35 a

1.36 c

1.37 h

1.38 i

1.39 d

1.40 a. His goodness and mercy shall follow me all the days of my life.
b. I will dwell in the house of the Lord forever.

1.41 a. Example:
My Father knows my needs and has promised to provide if I seek first His kingdom. Matt. 6:24-34
b. Example:
The Lord is faithful, who shall establish you, and keep you from evil. 2 Thessalonians 3:3

1.42 c. Example:
He has gone to prepare a place for me and promised to come back for me. John 14:1-3

1.42 teacher check

1.43 a. 5   e. 11
b. 6   f. 11
c. 10   g. 13
d. 10   h. 16

1.44 Example:
God does not allow testing of His servants to destroy them, but to strengthen them and increase them.

1.45 a. Vs.75 ". . .and that thou in faithfulness hast afflicted me."
b. Example:
comfort, rejoicing, new insights, new opportunities

1.46 teacher check

II. SECTION TWO

2.1 Abraham

2.2 heirs of promise

2.3 as a confirmation and an end of all strife

2.4 by Himself

2.5 Surely blessing I will bless thee, and multiplying I will multiply thee.

2.6 Example:
a strong consolation and a hope (Jesus) set before us an anchor of the soul

2.7 God's counsel, and God's oath

2.8 strong consolation

2.9 Hint:
life eternal in Jesus Christ (see Titus 3:7)

2.10 anchor of the soul

2.11　a. sure
　　　 b. steadfast

2.12　abideth faithful

2.13　I have sworn

2.14　nor suffer my faithfulness to fail

2.15　ever mindful

2.16　keepeth truth forever

2.17　there hath not failed one word

2.18　every purpose of the Lord shall be performed

2.19　not one jot or tittle shall pass from the Law

2.20　Examples:
　　　 a. forgiveness of sins and iniquities
　　　 b. no condemnation to those in Christ
　　　 c. everlasting life for those who hear and believe
　　　 d. wisdom given liberally if we ask
　　　 e. answered prayer if in accord with His will
　　　 f. help in temptation; no unbearable temptation
　　　 g. peace will keep our heart through Christ Jesus
　　　 h. fruitfulness if we abide in Christ
　　　 i. no one can "pluck" us out of Christ
　　　 j. prepared place so we can be with Him

2.21　teacher check

2.22　Any order:
　　　 a. They are works of men's hands.
　　　 b. They have mouths that don't speak.
　　　 c. They have eyes that don't see.
　　　 d. They have ears that don't hear.
　　　 e. They have noses that can't smell.
　　　 f. They have hands that can't handle.
　　　 g. They have throats that can't speak (make a noise).
　　　 h. They have feet that can't walk.

2.23　Any order:
　　　 a. he was talking or
　　　 b. he was pursuing or
　　　 c. he was in a journey or
　　　 d. he was sleeping or
　　　 e. (maybe) he is no god

2.24　Examples:
　　　 a. All man-made gods have the same weakness as their makers.
　　　 b. All men become like the gods they worship.

2.25　a. Numbers 22:5-41 Balaam—tried to... prophecy against Israel
　　　 b. I Samuel 13:5-14 Saul—tried to fill the role of a priest
　　　 c. John 18:1-5 Judas—betrayed his Lord
　　　 d. Joshua 7:18-26 Achan—took of the devoted spoils of Jericho
　　　 e. Genesis 4:1-18 Cain—wouldn't bring required offering

2.26　Examples; any order:
　　　 a. Joseph—he did not sin against God in Potiphar's house.
　　　 b. Moses—chose to suffer affliction with the people of God, rather than enjoy the pleasures of sin for a season
　　　 c. David—man after God's own heart
　　　 d. Abraham—believed God, counted as righteousness
　　　 e. Daniel—purposed not to defile himself

2.27　Examples; any order:
　　　 a. Salvation
　　　 b. Daily Provision
　　　 c. Comfort
　　　 d. Strength
　　　 e. Restoration

2.28　teacher check

2.29　teacher check

2.30　teacher check

III.　SECTION THREE

3.1　Any order:
　　　 a. uphold-The Lord upholdeth the righteous　　Ps. 37:17
　　　 b. direct-But the Lord directeth his steps Prov. 16:9
　　　 c. dispose-He removeth Kings, and setteth up Kings, Dan. 2:21
　　　 d. govern-Thou shalt judge the people righteously and govern the nations upon the earth Ps. 67:4

3.2 Joseph's brothers meant it for evil but God meant it for good.

3.3 Wicked men crucified the Lord Jesus but it was God's plan that He should die, but that death should not be able to hold Him.

3.4 a. The ground is cursed for Adam's sake; he must toil hard to make a living.
b. Unconditional
c. Man must work hard for his bread and must die.

3.5 a. God would never again destroy the world with water; ground no longer cursed; man would be feared by all beasts
b. Unconditional
c. Example: Rainbow still the sign of God's faithfulness

3.6 a. Make a great nation; bless thee; make thy name great; thou shalt be a blessing; bless them that bless thee; in thee all nations of the earth are blessed
b. Unconditional
c. Example: God sent Abraham a son; Jesus was the son of Abraham and the promised blessing.

3.7 a. The Law
b. Conditional
c. Example: Israel disobeyed–nation dispersed

3.8 a. He would have an everlasting kingdom
b. Unconditional
c. Example: Christ, the son of David, sits on His Father's right hand

3.9 adult check

3.10 My record is true–even though I bear record of myself–because I know where I came from and where I am going.

3.11 My judgment is true–for I am not alone, but I and the Father that sent me.

3.12 I bear witness of myself and The Father that sent me beareth witness of me.

3.13 He that sent me is true, and I speak to the world those things which I have heard.

3.14 As the Father taught me, I speak these things. I do nothing of myself.

3.15 If ye continue in my word ye shall know the truth and the truth shall set you free.

3.16 I speak that which I have seen with my Father.

3.17 A man that hath told you the truth, which I have heard of God.

3.18 Which of you convinceth me of sin? And if I say the truth, why do ye not believe me?

3.19 I know Him and keep His sayings, I would be a liar like you not to say so.

3.20 Same honor

3.21 Life in Father/Son

3.22 Know me you would have known the Father

3.23 You love the Father, you love me; I came from God

3.24 He that hath seen me hath seen the Father

3.25 In the Father and the Father in me

3.26 Jesus' works are God's works or same as

3.27 You hate the Father, you hate me

3.28 Any order:
  a. First begotten from the dead
  b. Prince of kings of the earth
  c. Loved us and washed us from our sins with His own blood.

3.29 teacher check

3.30 Examples; any order:
  a. Paid tithes/Received tithes
  b. Carnal commandment/Power an endless life
  c. Makes nothing perfect/Makes perfect
  d. Without an oath/With an oath
  e. Priest dies/Never dies
  f. Faulty-incomplete/Perfect-complete
  g. Animal offerings/Offered Himself
  h. Sanctuary made with hands/Sanctuary made without hands
  i. First covenant—faulty Second covenant—perfect
  j. Repeated sacrifice/Only one sacrifice

3.31 teacher check

3.32 a. vs. 11 Holy Father, keep through thine own name those whom thou hast given me, that they may be one, as we are.
  b. vs. 15 I pray -that thou shouldst keep them from the evil(evil one).
  c. vs. 17 Sanctify them through thy truth: thy word is truth.
  d. vs. 21 That they all may be one; as thou, Father, art in me, and I in thee, that they also may be in us.
  e. vs. 24 Father, I will that they also, whom thou hast given me, be with me where I am, and behold my glory
  f. vs. 26 That the love wherewith thou has loved me may be in them, and I in them.

IV. SECTION FOUR

4.1 Examples; any order:
  a. Abel/a more excellent sacrifice
  b. Enoch/he pleased God
  c. Noah/prepared an ark

  d. Abraham/went to a place he didn't know
  e. Sarah/believed God was faithful
  f. Isaac/blessed Jacob and Esau
  g. Jacob/blessed Joseph and two sons
  h. Joseph/mentioned the departing of Israel
  i. Moses/chose to suffer affliction with God's people
  j. Moses' parents/hid three months
  k. Rahab/received spies with peace
  l. Gideon, Barak, Jephthah, David, Samuel, and the prophets/obedience to God

4.2 Examples:
  a. Word was in the beginning 1:1
  b. Word was with God 1:1
  c. Word was God 1:1
  d. Word was made flesh 1:14
  e. Word dwelt among us 1:14
  f. the Son hath declared the Father 1:18
  g. the sent one (Jesus) speaks the words of God 3:34
  h. hearing the word and believing yields eternal life 5:24
  i. the words of Christ are spirit and life 6:63
  j. continuing in His words is mark of disciple 8:31 or words are truth 8:32
  k. we have the word of reconcilation 2 Cor. 5:19
  l. the Word of God is the sword of the Spirit Eph. 6:17
  m. Word of God is alive Heb. 4:12
  n. Word of God is powerful 4:12
  o. Word of God is sharper than two-edged sword 4:12 or pierces to dividing asunder of soul and spirit 4:12 or discerner of thoughts and intents of the heart 4:12

4.3 Servant is always to be ready to receive his master when he comes even though he doesn't know the time.

4.4 Unfaithfulness in stewardship will be found out. You cannot serve two masters. If we can't be trusted with little things, how can we be trusted with large things?

4.5 After we have done all that we are supposed to do we are still unprofitable servants. We have just done our duty.

4.6 The amount of stewardship will differ but the principle of faithfulness is the same for all. God will reward faithfulness and will not overlook unfaithfulness in stewardship.

4.7 Stewards of opportunity—We will have to give an account of opportunities given and our treatment of those whom God has sent, particularly His Son.

4.8 a. righteousness
b. love His appearing

4.9 a. incorruptible
b. running well

4.10 a. life
b. endureth temptation, or love for the Lord

4.11 a. glory
b. leadership

4.12 a. life
b. being faithful unto death

1.1	e
1.2	c
1.3	a
1.4	m
1.5	h
1.6	d
1.7	f
1.8	n
1.9	k
1.10	i
1.11	l
1.12	b
1.13	g or a
1.14	j
1.15	Augustus
1.16	Tiberius
1.17	A.D. 37-A.D. 41
1.18	A.D. 41-A.D. 54
1.19	Nero
1.20	false
1.21	false
1.22	true
1.23	false
1.24	true
1.25	true
1.26	Caligula
1.27	Claudius
1.28	Tiberius
1.29	Augustus

1.30	Augustus
1.31	true
1.32	true
1.33	false
1.34	true
1.35	false
1.36	false
1.37	Mediterranean Sea
1.38	Greek
1.39	paying taxes
1.40	senate
1.41	procurator
1.42	senatorial aristocracy
1.43	equestrian
1.44	emancipated slaves
1.45	plebes
1.46	slaves
1.47	land
1.48	mining, or trade, or agriculture
1.49	agriculture or animal husbandry or (mining, or trade)
1.50	Scriptures
1.51	forum
1.52	Greeks
1.53	governmental

1.54 Senatorial aristocracy

1.55 Equestrian order

1.56 Freedmen (emancipated slaves)

1.57 Plebes

1.58 Slaves

1.59 tunica

1.60 toga

1.61 stola

1.62 teacher check

1.63 syncretism

1.64 Greeks

1.65 pantheism (pantheistic)

1.66 form

1.67 Jewish synagogue

1.68 Jewish sect

1.69 Caesar (the emperor)

1.70 Jews

1.71 The emperor was the most powerful person alive and controlled the destinies of all those in the Roman Empire.

1.72 They were required to show reverence to the emperor himself or to an image of him, whether a life-sized statue or a portrait. They were expected to bow in adoration when he passed by in a parade. Nero and Gaius (Caligula) required the people to make a sacrifice to them.

1.73 Gallio was totally indifferent to the accusations and actions of the Jews (Acts 18:12-16).

1.74 He recognized Paul's innocence and gave Paul liberty and protection from the Jews. For two years he kept Paul guarded, and talked with him often. He was quite impressed with Paul. He referred final judgment to Porcius Festus (Acts 24:22-27).

1.75 c. the founding of a popular apostle

1.76 b. Romans present in Jerusalem on the Day of Pentecost

1.77 a. the lower classes of the empire

1.78 d. Gentiles

1.79 c. a synagogue

1.80 a. to worship God
b. for the exercise of discipline
c. for mutual edification
d. for the carrying forward of Christian service

1.81 a. prayer
b. singing of psalms
c. exercising the gifts of the Spirit
d. reading and expounding the Scriptures

1.82 When they were banished from Rome under the Emperor Claudius, they went to Corinth where they lived and worked with Paul for one and one-half years. When they moved back to Rome, they became teachers and sponsored a church in their home.

1.83 third

1.84 Nero

1.85 Gaius

1.86 Second Corinthians

1.87 A.D. 57-58

1.88 Spain

1.89 a. to establish the Romans in the fundamental doctrines of Christianity
b. to protect the Romans from Judaizing influence
c. to acquaint them with his desire to use Rome as a base for his outreach to Spain
d. to secure financial support of the Romans for his outreach to Spain

1.90 She had already planned to visit Rome, so Paul took the opportunity to ask if she would deliver the letter. The empire had no postal system except for official government business. Personal letters had to be carried by friends or special messengers.

1.91 Paul had been making a collection for the Jerusalem church as he traveled through Greece and Asia Minor. He hoped that the collection would also relieve suspicions of him and his work because some of the Jewish Christians in Jerusalem were wary of him. The collection was completed, and Paul wanted to personally present the gifts.

1.92 d. a, b, and c

1.93 d. Spain

1.94 c. sin and God's solution to it

1.95 b. a "Gospel Manifesto"

1.96 Judaizers

1.97 Israel

1.98 others in the body of Christ

1.99 higher authorities

1.100 salvation

1.101 He was preparing to embark on a new missionary territory, facing new problems and trials. He may have been conscious of a turning point in his life as a result. He must have intended this letter to be a concise summary and restatement of his basic thinking as an instructional tool for establishing believers in the fundamental doctrine of salvation.

II. SECTION TWO

2.1 servant of Jesus Christ

2.2 Jesus

2.3 a. called
b. apostle

2.4 all that be in Rome

2.5 any person made righteous by the saving blood of Jesus Christ

2.6 Coming out from anything that is not in keeping with the perfect will of God. When we leave something for the sake of the Gospel, He moves us into a more glorious position. We are separated to live and proclaim the good news of Jesus Christ. Anything contrary to such a life is not complete separation.

2.7 Check with illustration on page 19.

2.8 b. edification

2.9 c. establish churches

2.10 d. in Jesus

2.11 a. teach all nations

2.12 c. establish learners in the basic principles of life

2.13 Romans 1:16-17; "For I am not ashamed of the gospel of Christ: for it is the power of God unto salvation to every one that believeth; to the Jew first, and also to the Greek. For therein is the righteousness of God revealed from faith to faith: as it is written, The just shall live by faith."

2.14   good news

2.15   the atoning work of Jesus accomplished at Calvary and evidenced by His Resurrection

2.16   by hearing the gospel

2.17   Paul had seen the risen Lord and had become consumed with the Lord's purpose of salvation and with establishing believers in His doctrine.

2.18   d. everyone

2.19   c. through Adam

2.20   b. man ignored God's obvious Law

2.21   a. they become reprobate

2.22   c. God's goodness

2.23   c. one whose heart is circumcised

2.24   Hint:
Use the following scripture references: Genesis 19:1-10; Judges 19:22-26 and 20:13; Leviticus 18:22; 1 Corintians 6:9; 1 Timothy 1:10; and Romans 1:23-32.

2.25   Hint:
See 1 Corinthians 7:9 and 1 John 1:5-9

2.26   self-contained; totally independent of God's mercy and love; self-governing

2.27   a change of mind which leads to a change in behaviour

2.28   depraved, rejected of God, damned

2.29   a. according to truth; Romans 2:2
b. according to a person's deeds; Romans 2:6
c. according to the Law; Romans 2:12
d. according to God's Gospel; Romans 2:14

2.30   Examples:
a. Jesus
lay on others heavy burdens to carry, but won't lift a finger to help them
Paul
know His will, yet approve of things not in His will
b. Jesus
all their works they do to be seen of men: broadened phylacteries, large borders on garments, uppermost rooms at feasts, chief seats in the synogogue, greetings in the market, and to be called Rabbi.
Paul
are confident that thou art a guide of the blind, a light of them which are in darkness, an instructor of the foolish, a teacher of babes, which hast the form of knowledge and of the truth in the Law.
c. Jesus
shut up kingdom of heaven against men—neither go in, or allow others to enter
Paul
thou that teachest others, teachest not thou thyself? thou that preachest a man should not steal dost thou steal?
d. Jesus
devour widows' houses, and for pretense make long prayers
Paul
thou that sayest a man should not commit adultery dost thou commit adultery? thou that abhorest idols, dost thou commit sacrilege?
e. Jesus
compass sea and land to make one proselyte and then make him twofold more the child of hell than themselves

Paul
Thou that makest thy boast of
the Law, through breaking the
Law dishonorest thou God?

f. Jesus
blind guides who say "Whosoever
shall swear by the temple, it is
nothing; but whosoever shall
swear by the gold of the
temple, he is a debtor
Paul
The name of God is blasphemed
among the Gentiles through you.

g. Jesus
pay tithe of mint, and anise,
and cummin, and have omitted
the matters of Law, judgment,
mercy, and faith
Paul
Therefore if the uncircumcision
keep the righteousness of the Law,
shall not his uncircumcision be
counted for circumcision?

h. Jesus
strain at a gnat and swallow a
camel
Paul
And shall not uncircumcision which
is by nature, if it fulfill the
the Law, judge thee who by the
letter and circumcision dost
transgress the Law?

i. Jesus
make the outside of the cup or
platter clean, but within they
are full of extortion and excess
Paul
But he is a Jew, which is one
inwardly; and circumcision is that
of the heart, in the spirit and
not in the letter; whose praise
is not of men, but of God.

2.31 grace

2.32 propitiation

2.33 justification

2.34 guilt

2.35 redeem

2.36 atonement

2.37 faith

2.38 remission

2.39 Abraham

2.40 to miss the mark

2.41 They were called forth to pave the
way for God's plan of redemption.

2.42 to make men aware of their sinful
condition

2.43 It was not a covenant made between
equal parties, but was a gracious
gift of God.

2.44 faith in God and acting on His
provision of forgiveness and
abundant life

2.45 The teaching proposed that Gentiles
must become Jewish proselytes and
be circumcised before they could
become Christians.

2.46 He stated the fact that the rite
of circumcision was a result of
faith in God which was credited
as his righteousness—faith came
before circumcision.

2.47 He knew God's promises were sure.

2.48 a. righteousness 4:3
b. inheritance 4:13
c. posterity 4:17

2.49 those who "believe on Him that raised up Jesus our Lord from the dead,
Who was delivered for our offenses,
and was raised again for our
justification"

2.50 Any five; any order; examples:
a. peace
b. access to God's grace
c. hope of glory
d. rejoicing
e. glory in tribulations or patience,
experience, hope, love of God

2.51 false

2.52 true

2.53 false

2.54 false

2.55 true

2.56 false

2.57 true

2.58 true

2.59 true

2.60 false

2.61 disobedience and offense

2.62 from one–second Adam (Jesus Christ)

2.63 brought righteousness and life

2.64 brought sin and death

2.65 unto all; many

2.66 the union with Christ in His death and Resurrection

2.67 We should walk in newness of life.

2.68 a. saved by Jesus' life
b. grace abounded unto many
c. the righteous shall reign in life
d. grace abounded more than sin

2.69 Example: According to Romans 6:15-23, a person has a choice of serving one of two masters–sin or God. Man does not choose whether or not he will be a servant, but whom he will serve. If he chooses to serve sin, the wages are impurity, greater iniquity, and finally death. If he chooses to serve God, the wages include sanctification, righteousness, and eternal life. By faith in Jesus we can learn to master sin and become love-slaves of God through Jesus Christ.

2.70 b. marriage

2.71 c. adultery

2.72 d. accept justification through Jesus

2.73 a. provoked

2.74 c. condemned or b. schooled

2.75 Example: The law is spiritual, but man is carnal. Therefore, it is impossible for carnal man to live a spiritual life by his own efforts. He must rely on the Spirit of God.

2.76 gratification of selfish and evil desires

2.77 allowing the Holy Spirit to work in a person's life, keeping him from sin and aiding him in weakness

2.78 a. condemnation
b. death
c. Abba, Father
d. sufferings, glory
e. sons of God
f. pray
g. good
h. against us
i. conquerors
j. separate; love

III. SECTION THREE

3.1 Adam

3.2 sin

3.3 heart

3.4 to do wrong, commit any kind of offense, or have any faults; sin is anything short of perfect holiness

3.5 the infallible Word of God

3.6 "For all have sinned and come short of the glory of God."

3.7 Example: We are tempted in an area of weakness. As we dwell on the act, we make a decision to refuse it or fulfill it. When the act of sin is committed, death wins a victory.

3.7 Con't.
For instance, an overweight person sees a chocolate fudge cake. The more he thinks about that cake, the more he wants it. Finally, he eats it, and once again loses the battle of the bulge and increases the pressure on his heart.

3.8 Any three; any order:
a. hiding from God; fear
b. Adam blames God for the woman
c. the woman blames the serpent
d. by the fig leaves they were trying to cover for their sin or Adam sinned knowingly after Eve was deceived.

3.9 a. sin

3.10 c. 70-80

3.11 b. 969

3.12 d. nature

3.13 b. a great gulf

3.14 d. unable

3.15 "For the wages of sin is death; but the gift of God is eternal life through Jesus Christ our Lord."

3.16 a. man from the presence of God
b. obtain spiritual life through faith in the Lord Jesus Christ (Romans 6:23)

3.17 a. the spirit and soul from the body
b. Jesus shall destroy the last enemy, or death (1 Cor. 15:27), and the corruptible shall put on immortality. Death will be swallowed up in victory (vs. 54).

3.18 a. man from God forever
b. There is none. Once one enters hell, there is no chance of returning to the presence of God.

3.19 The natural inclination is to find the remedy for sin within one's self, attempting to secure salvation through human means.

3.20 a blood sacrifice - Hebrews 9:22

3.21 Only Jesus was the Lamb without spot or blemish. God required a perfect sacrifice, so it had to be His only Son.

3.22 Instead of justice, God extended his mercy so that we could be saved. Not according to our own righteousness, but according to the free gift of God through Jesus Christ, we can be cleansed, regenerated, and renewed by the Holy Ghost.

3.23 Example:
Jesus came to this earth, not to condemn, but to redeem the people of God's affection. Love is why He came. Refer to Roman 5:8; John 3:16-17; 2 Cor. 5:21; Gal. 2:20; Eph. 2:4-5; 1 John 3:1; Eph. 5:2; 1 John 4:16; and any others pertaining to the love of God.

3.24 "But God commendeth His love toward us; in that, while we were yet sinners, Christ died for us."

3.25 c. Nicodemus

3.26 d. believes in the atoning work of Jesus' blood

3.27 a. to intellectually accept

3.28 b. the blood

3.29 a. Confess with thy mouth the Lord Jesus;
b. Believe in thine heart that God hath raised him from the dead.

3.30 Any order:
a. quick
b. powerful
c. sharper than any two-edged sword
d. discerner of thoughts and intents of the heart or piercing even to the dividing asunder of soul and spirit

3.31 "For I am not ashamed of the gospel of Christ: for it is the power of God unto salvation to every one that believeth; to the Jew first, and also to the Greek. For therein is the righteousness of God revealed from faith to faith: as it is written, The just shall live by faith."

3.32 "Therefore being justified by faith, we have peace with God through our Lord Jesus Christ."

3.33 Example:
Andrew's solution to any event was "take it to Jesus." He first brought his brother to meet Jesus. Then he presented what was available for Jesus' use. He led groups of people to Jesus.

3.34 Example:
Atonement is accomplished through the blood sacrifice of a perfect offering. Our atonement was achieved by the perfect Lamb of God's sacrificial blood being poured out on the altar. Refer to such Scriptures as: Romans 3:25; 5:9; Eph. 1:7; Lev. 17:11 and 1 Peter 1:19.

3.35 c. Christ's righteousness

3.36 c. totally unrighteous

3.37 d. separation from sin

3.38 wisdom, righteousness, sanctification, and redemption

3.39 Example:
To reckon means to *consider as*, to *regard as being*.
If we consider ourselves dead to sin, we act on the fact that sin has no hold on us. Rather than giving in to temptation, we recall the fact that Jesus has made a way of escape through His atonement. We consider ourselves alive to Christ in that we do all things as unto His glory and honor and allow Jesus to live His victorious life through us. (Gal. 2:20)

3.40 "Likewise reckon ye also yourselves to be dead indeed to sin, but alive unto God through Jesus Christ our Lord."

3.41 d. to the uttermost

3.42 b. interceding for us

3.43 c. preserved

3.44 "There is therefore now no condemnation to them which are in Christ Jesus, who walk not after the flesh, but after the Spirit."

3.45 Romans 1:1-17—Salutation
Romans 1:18-2:29—Downward spiral of sin
Romans 3—Universal sin and guilt, emphasizing the Jewish nation
Romans 4—Abraham
Romans 5—Justification
Romans 6—Reckoning justification by baptism
Romans 7—Carnal nature vs. spiritual nature
Romans 8—Life in the Holy Spirit

1.1   a synagogue

1.2   He prayed to be punished in place of his people.

1.3   Isaac

1.4   the characteristic of being supreme in power, rank, and authority

1.5   Hosea and Isaiah

1.6   Any order:
   a. the adoption (sonship)
   b. the glory
   c. the covenants
   d. the giving of the Law
   e. the service of God
   f. the promises
   g. the patriarchal heritage
   h. the Messiah

1.7   a. circumcised on the 8th day
   b. of the stock of Israel
   c. of the tribe of Benjamin
   d. a Hebrew of the Hebrews
   e. as touching the Law, a Pharisee
   f. concerning zeal, persecuting the church
   g. touching the righteousness which is in the Law, blameless

1.8   Any order:
   a. "to be conformed to the image of His Son"
   b. to be justified and glorified
   c. to be adopted and accepted in the beloved, Jesus Christ
   d. "that we be to the praise of his glory, who first trusted in Christ."

1.9   knowledge

1.10   the Law

1.11   faultlessly obeying it (which is impossible)

1.12   Jesus Christ

1.13   the house of Israel

1.14   our mouths and hearts

1.15   a. confess with our mouth the Lord Jesus
   b. believe in our hearts that God raised Him from the dead

1.16   Any order:
   a. Someone must be sent by God.
   b. They must hear the Gospel.
   c. They must hear from a preacher.
   d. They must believe on the Lord.

1.17   Example:
   Men desire to be self-sufficient, independent of help or wise counsel. To live by faith is to abandon one's sense of autonomy and depend on God for righteousness.

1.18   Elijah

1.19   He caused them not to see or hear.

1.20   in order to bring salvation to the Gentiles

1.21   They should not boast against the Jews or they will also be cut off.

1.22   When the fullness of the Gentiles comes in, Israel will be restored to the Gospel.

1.23 Example:
Paul was a Jew by birth, but his ministry was mainly to carry the Gospel to the Gentiles. He saw both sides, and therefore had the authority to call the Jews to repentance and to admonish Gentile Christians to remain humble, remembering that they were grafted into God's promises to the Jews.

1.24 b

1.25 d

1.26 a

1.27 c

1.28 a. Chapter 1 Salutation and downward spiral of sin
b. Chapter 2 Downward spiral of sin
c. Chapter 3 Universal sin and guilt, emphasis on Jews
d. Chapter 4 Abraham
e. Chapter 5 Justification
f. Chapter 6 Reckoning justification by baptism
g. Chapter 7 Carnal nature vs. spiritual nature
h. Chapter 8 Life in the Holy Spirit
i. Chapter 9 God's sovereignty
j. Chapter 10 Jewish unbelief
k. Chapter 11 Grafting of the Gentiles

II. SECTION TWO

2.1 to present our bodies before God as a living sacrifice

2.2 by the renewing of our minds; having God change our attitudes, motives, etc.

2.3 everyone of God's children

2.4 in the body of Christ

2.5 love

2.6 deed and in truth

2.7 heaven on earth

2.8 ye have done it unto me

2.9 attitude and motive behind it

2.10 a worshipful relationship with Jesus Christ

2.11 but overcome evil with good

2.12 Any order:
a. word of wisdom
b. word of knowledge
c. faith
d. gifts of healing
e. working of miracles
f. prophecy
g. discerning of spirits
h. diverse kinds of tongues
i. interpretation of tongues

2.13 Any order:
a. prophecy
b. ministry
c. teaching
d. exhorting
e. giving
f. ruling
g. showing mercy

2.14 for the edification of the entire body of Christ

2.15 they are ordained of God

2.16 His children

2.17 resist the ordinance of God

2.18 law and force

2.19 love and service

2.20 obey the law (or do that which is good)

2.21 not obey God's higher laws by which Christians are to live

2.22 obey or yield to higher authority

2.23 God

2.24 God's ministers

2.25 occupy this earth until Jesus comes to establish his kingdom

2.26 submission to God

2.27 love

2.28 a. love
b. praise
c. prayer
d. intercession

2.29 teacher check

2.30 to insist that Gentiles not eat meat, drink wine, and reverence the Sabbath

2.31 They could not distinguish whether or not it had been used to make sacrifices to idols.

2.32 They were commemorating Jesus' Resurrection Day.

2.33 a. The narrow view follows a list of do's and don't's and calls others "liberalists."
b. The broader view sees no transgressions among their lists and calls others "legalists."

2.34 He promoted a more comprehensive view which calls upon each person's convictions and allows others to do so.

2.35 Jewish punctilliousness

2.36 We are to judge that "no man put a stumbling block or an occasion to fall in his brother's way."

2.37 conviction (14:5) conscience (14:22) and consideration (15:1-2)

2.38 Gentiles

2.39 Spain

2.40 love

2.41 one or perfect in one

III. SECTION THREE

3.1 **everyone or all**

3.2 "The heart is deceitful above all things, and desperately wicked."

3.3 Gen. 3:15

3.4 that Jesus would be born of a virgin, and that he would have final victory over Satan

3.5 the Roman Christian's feet (and ours)

3.6 death; or a blood sacrifice

3.7 He killed innocent animals to clothe them with skins.

3.8 Both the earth and the human heart were covered in darkness until God sent the Holy Spirit to move us out of the void and bring us to salvation.

3.9 receiving Jesus Christ as Saviour

3.10 Example:
Original sin is the inherent sinfulness of all mankind referring to the basic motivations behind all we say, think, and do. It includes the concept that man's will is diametrically opposed to the will of God.

3.11 "For whosoever shall call upon the name of the Lord shall be saved."

3.12 "That thou shalt confess with thy mouth the Lord Jesus, and shalt believe in thine heart that God hath raised him from the dead, thou shalt be saved. For with the heart man believeth unto righteousness; and with the mouth confession is made unto salvation."

3.13 "The spirit itself beareth witness with our spirit, that we are the children of God."

3.14 false

3.15 true

3.16 true

3.17 true

3.18 false

3.19 our willingness to trust God and follow the leading of the spirit

3.20 something that causes distress, sorrow, affliction or misery

3.21 heard his cry and enlarged him

3.22 joy of the Lord

3.23 to be a praise to the glory of God

3.24 temptation

3.25 the Holy Spirit

3.26 Any order:
a. prayer
b. using God's provision of Christian armor
c. confession of God's Word (provisions of deliverance) or assert our dominion over the bondage of sin through Jesus

3.27 "But put ye on the Lord Jesus Christ, and make not provision for the flesh, to fulfill the lusts thereof."

3.28 "So then faith cometh by hearing, and hearing by the word of God."

3.29 "And we know that all things work together for good to them that love God, to them who are the called according to his purpose."

3.30 "He that spared not his own Son, but delivered him up for us all, how shall he not with him also freely give us all things."

3.31 Example:
Temptation of pre-marital sexual relationships: Ephesians 5:3 "But fornication, and all uncleaness, or covetousness, let it not once be named among you, as becometh saints."
1 Thessalonians 4:3 "For this is the will of God, even your sanctification, that ye should abstain from fornication."
1 Corinthians 6:13, 18-20 "...Now the body is not for fornication, but for the Lord: and the Lord for the body." "Flee fornication. Every sin that a man doeth is without the body; but he that committeth fornication sinneth against his own body. What? Know ye not that your body is the temple of the Holy Ghost..."

3.32 our faith

3.33 believeth that Jesus is the Son of God

3.34 a. Jesus
b. Him as He is

3.35   that God is able to bring
       redemption, healing, wholeness and
       salvation to everyone who
       believes in Jesus Christ

3.36   by the blood of the Lamb and the
       testimony of the saints

3.37   a. His Word
       b. praise and worship
       c. prayer

3.38   Any order:
       a. We are given to eat of the
          tree of life in the paradise
          of God.
       b. We shall not be hurt in the
          second death.
       c. We will be given power over
          the nations.
       d. We will be clothed in white
          raiment and our names
          confessed before God & the
          angels.
       e. We will be made a pillar in
          the temple and have written
          on us the name of God,
          Jerusalem, and Jesus' new
          name.
       f. We will be allowed to sit
          with Jesus in his throne.

3.39   "I beseech you therefore,
       brethren, by the mercies of
       God, that ye present your
       bodies a living sacrifice, holy,
       acceptable unto God, which is
       your reasonable service. And
       be not conformed to this world:
       but be ye transformed by the
       renewing of your mind, that ye
       may prove what is that good,
       and acceptable, and perfect,
       will of God."

3.40   "Nay, in all these things we
       are more than conquerors through
       him that loved us."

1.1   teacher check

1.2   e

1.3   j

1.4   d

1.5   i

1.6   c

1.7   h or j

1.8   g

1.9   b

1.10   a

1.11   f

1.12   glutton, drunkard, friend of publicans and sinners

1.13   Sabbath breaker

1.14   deceiver, a good man

1.15   demon-possessed, a Samaritan

1.16   sinner

1.17   Any order:
- a. Lord
- b. Jesus
- c. Christ
- d. Son of God
- e. (Son) of David
- f. God
- g. Emmanuel
- h. Savior

1.18   teacher check

1.19   teacher check

1.20   e

1.21   g

1.22   h

1.23   f

1.24   a

1.25   c

1.26   d

1.27   Nestorius

1.28   Eutychus

1.29   Cerinthus and Ebionites

1.30   Docetics

1.31   Apollinarius

1.32   Arius and Jehovah's Witnesses

1.33   Socinianism/Unitarians

1.34   Examples:
- a. The Kenosis - He emptied himself of the manifestation of his divine glory and the independent use of certain divine attributes.
- b. The virgin birth - He was conceived by the Holy Spirit and born of the virgin Mary.

1.35   Any order:
- a. eternal
- b. immutable
- c. omnipotent
- d. omniscient
- e. omnipresent

1.36   Examples; any order:
- a. creation
- b. miracles
- c. receiving worship
- d. forgiving sins
- e. resurrecting his people
- f. giving eternal life
- g. judging men

1.37   "And Jesus increased in wisdom and stature, and in favour with God and man."

2.1   Any order:
a. Prophet
b. Priest
c. King

2.2   Examples; any order:
a. to Jacob in a dream
b. in the fiery furnace
c. the burning bush
d. the call of Gideon

2.3   teacher check

2.4   Examples; any order:
a. His death was substitutionary.
b. His death provided redemption.
c. His death was both physical and spiritual.

2.5
a. governmental
b. commercial transaction
c. accident
d. substitution
e. ransom to Satan
f. martyr
g. love of God

2.6   b

2.7   e or b

2.8   a

2.9   c or e

2.10   "Forasmuch as ye know that ye were not redeemed with corruptible things, as silver and gold, from your vain conversation received by tradition from your fathers; But with the precious blood of Christ, as of a lamb without blemish and without spot:"

2.11   teacher check

2.12   Any order:
a. He did not die.
b. He was resurrected spiritually, not bodily.
c. the disciples were hallucinating

2.13   Any order:
a. central message of the church
b. essential for our salvation
c. validates Christ's person and work
d. guarantees our resurrection

2.14
a. High Priest
b. need
c. intercessor
d. temptation
e. Advocate
f. sin

2.15   teacher check

1.1   c. father of a nation

1.2   a. Ur

1.3   d. sovereignty

1.4   c. Genesis chapter 12

1.5   b. Sarah

1.6   c. Eliezar

1.7   c. Canaan

1.8   a. Isaac

1.9   d. circumcision

1.10   d. both a and b

1.11   a. Get thee out of thy country
       b. from thy kindred
       c. from thy father's house
       d. go to a land that I will show
          thee

1.12   Any order:
       a. God would make Abraham a great
          nation.
       b. God would bless him and make his
          name great.
       c. Abraham would become a blessing.
       d. God would bless those who blessed
          him and curse those who cursed him.
       e. Through Abraham all the families
          of the earth would be blessed.

1.13   vigorous, or the quality of living
       and growing with full vital strength

1.14   association, or the bringing together
       of persons into a relationship as
       companions, partners, or friends

1.15   a binding and solemn agreement made
       by two or more parties in which
       each party agrees to certain condi-
       tions

1.16   Five animals (except the birds) were
       cut in two while Abraham slept; a
       smoking furnace and a burning
       lamp passed between the pieces.

1.17   Example:
When the Perfect Sacrifice was laid before God on the Cross, a great darkness covered the earth so that even those who would benefit from the transaction taking place could not see the actual event. God and His Son made a covenant of eternal life and blessing for all the joint-heirs with Jesus, just as God made the Abrahamic Covenant with Himself, that blessing and great promises would come to Abraham and his heirs.

1.18   Goshen

1.19   triumph

1.20   judges

1.21   idolatry

1.22   Moab

1.23   Naomi

1.24   a. David
       b. Jesus

1.25   Samuel

1.26   a. Saul
       b. David

1.27   Rehoboam

1.28   Israel

1.29   Judah

1.30   Jeroboam

1.31   i

1.32   a

1.33   g

1.34   j

1.35   b

1.36   d

1.37   c

1.38   e

1.39   k

1.40   f

1.41   h

1.42   400

1.43   a. 539
       b. 334

1.44   333

1.45   323

1.46   320

1.47   a. 163
       b. 63

1.48   a. 8
       b. 25

1.49   Hellenistic culture

1.50   Egypt

1.51   Septuagint

1.52   Syria

1.53   Mattathias

1.54   "hammer"

1.55   Example:
       When the Syrians took control of
       Palestine, they were determined to
       enforce Hellenism upon the Jews.
       The Jews who favored the Greek
       style of life became opposed to the
       orthodox Jews, especially concerning
       the office of high priest. Antiochus
       Ephiphanes used this rivalry as an
       opportunity to destroy orthodox
       Judaism. He erected a statue of
       Jupiter in the Temple and used
       swine for a sacrifice. He also
       forbade the Jews to worship on the
       Sabbath, practice circumcision, or
       observe the feast days. Copies of
       the Scriptures were destroyed; and
       Jewish people were killed, beaten,
       or sold into slavery for their faith.
       Finally a priest named Mattathias,
       his five sons, and some followers
       rose in rebellion against the Syrians.

1.56   the scattering of the Jews after
       the Babylonian exile.

1.57   John the Baptist

1.58   Paul

1.59   a person who has been converted from
       one religion, opinion, or party to
       another.

1.60   "...until the fulness of the Gentiles
       be come in."

1.61   teacher check

II. SECTION TWO

2.1   false

2.2   true

2.3   true

2.4   true

2.5   false

2.6   false

2.7   true

2.8   false

2.9   true

2.10   true

2.11   false

2.12   Example:
       The Zealots were anti-Roman Jews
       opposed to paying taxes or in any
       way succumbing to Roman authority.
       They militantly favored and fought
       for Jewish independence.

2.13   Example:
       Hadrian decided to rebuild Jerusalem
       as a Greek city to be called Aelia
       Capitolina. This act caused fierce
       resentment among the Jews and
       instigated three and one-half years
       of war.

2.14 a. the first part of the Talmud, containing oral interpretations of Scriptural ordinances
      b. the second supplementary part of the Talmud, providing a commentary on the Mishna
      c. the collection of writings constituting the Jewish civil and religious law, consisting of two parts, the Mishna (text) and Gemara (commentary)

2.15 a. unity of God
      b. man's ability to approach God
      c. immortality of the soul
      d. recognition of many Jewish prophets
      e. Jerusalem as "spiritual headquarters"

2.16 Europe

2.17 wealth

2.18 ghettos

2.19 eighteenth

2.20 a. Germany
      b. France

2.21 Gotthold Lessing

2.22 Napoleon Bonaparte

2.23 New Amsterdam

2.24 Newport, Rhode Island

2.25 anti-Semitism

2.26 f

2.27 a

2.28 c

2.29 d

2.30 g

2.31 b

2.32 e

2.33 a. translation of the Pentateuch into German

      b. philosophic defense of Judaism
      c. encouragement to his Jewish brethren

2.34 Palestine

2.35 Arabs

2.36 Either order:
      a. the United States
      b. Britain

2.37 Either order:
      a. Roosevelt
      b. Churchhill

2.38 Either order:
      a. the United States
      b. the Soviet Union

2.39 Six Day War

2.40 Example:
      On this date, the UN General Assembly passed a resolution on the partition of Palestine. Jerusalem was to be an enclave, and the new Jewish and Arab states were to be linked in economic union.

2.41 Example:
      In Tel Aviv, at 4 p.m. on May 14, 1948, David Ben Gurion read the proclamation of independence. The state of Israel was born.

2.42 true

2.43 false

2.44 true

2.45 true

2.46 true

2.47 God the Father

2.48 Jesus the Son

2.49 the Holy Spirit

2.50 body of Christ

2.51 Jesus or the New Testament Church

2.52 Jesus, the high priest

2.53   Examples; any order:
   a. Both were preserved in childhood.
      (Ex. 2:2-10; Mt. 2:14, 15)
   b. Both contended with evil rulers.
      (Ex. 7:11; Mt. 4:1)
   c. Both fasted 40 days.(Ex. 34:28;
      Mt 4:2)
   d. Both were given the power to do
      miracles as proof of their
      ministry.
   e. Both carried out their ministry
      in hostile surroundings.
   f. Both spoke to the people of a
      promised land.(Canaan; Kingdom
      of Heaven)
   g. Both surrendered their position
      of royalty for their ministry to
      the people.
   h. Both had seventy helpers.(Num 11:16
      and 17; Lk. 10:1)
   i. Both instructed the people from
      a mountain.(Moses read law;
      Jesus' Sermon on the Mount)
   j. Both had radiant faces.(Ex. 34:35;
      Mt. 17:2)

2.54   Examples; any order:
   a. Both were their father's favorite
      son.
   b. Both were sent by their fathers
      to care for their brethren.
   c. Both were sold for pieces of
      silver.
   d. Both were falsely accused by
      their brethren.
   e. Both were counted as outlaws.
   f. Both made no defense when falsely
      accused.
   g. Both became servants in a strange
      land.
   h. Both had special coats which were
      parted among brethren by casting
      lots.(Genesis 37:33 and John 19:24)
   i. Both were exalted to the throne
      as saviors of the world.
   j. Both were given new names.

III. SECTION THREE

3.1   Moabite Stone

3.2   Rosetta Stone

3.3   Moabite Stone

3.4   Behistun Inscription

3.5   Amarna Letters

3.6   Rosetta Stone

3.7   Behistun Inscription

3.8   Behistun Inscription

3.9   Rosetta Stone

3.10   Amarna Letters

3.11   Babylonians

3.12   library

3.13   Nuzi

3.14   Horites

3.15   Mari Letters

3.16   Hoshiah

3.17   e

3.18   a

3.19   g

3.20   b

3.21   f

3.22   d

3.23   The Code of Hammurabi provides
       background material for bodies of
       law including the Laws of Moses
       recorded in the Pentateuch.

3.24   The Ras Shamra Tablets exposed the
       extreme wickedness of the Canaanite
       religion in the areas of violence
       and sexual immorality.

3.25   Example:
       The Nuzi Tablets explain the fact
       that a trusted servant could become
       an heir if the householder had no
       son. Thus, Abraham was willing to
       adopt Eliezer as his heir if God
       did not grant him a child by natural
       means. Another custom was that
       of giving a handmaid to a new
       bride, as was the case with Rachel

3.26 The discoveries at Mari included (1) the temple of Ishtar, the Babylonian fertility goddess; (2) the royal palace, a huge building beautifully decorated; and (3) the Mari Letters, some twenty thousand clay tablets found in the royal archines.

3.27 These twenty-one letters were written during the time when the Babylonian Empire was overrunning Palestine, just before the destruction of Jerusalem, and during the time when Jeremiah was warning the people of Judah's doom.

3.28 1947

3.29 goat herders

3.30 Either order:
a. Lankester Harding
b. Pere R. de Vaux

3.31 ten

3.32 Old Testament

3.33 Isaiah

3.34 Essenes

3.35 Khirbet Qumran

3.36 Example:
The scroll of Isaiah was the first major Biblical manuscript of great antiquity ever to be recovered. It predated by a millenium the oldest Hebrew text preserved in the Masoretic Hebrew Bible. The Mazorite Bible has been the basis of all recent translations, but does not go back any earlier than A.D. 900.

3.37 a

3.38 c

3.39 a

3.40 d

3.41 d

3.42 a

3.43 c

3.44 b

3.45 d

3.46 a

3.47 Bethlehem

3.48 Constantine's mother, Helena

3.49 Caesarea

3.50 Caesar Augustus

3.51 Capernaum

3.52 Caesarea

3.53 Antioch

3.54 "Queen of the East"

3.55 agoras

3.56 Corinth

3.57 Ephesus

3.58 three

3.59 temple of Diana

3.60 Any order:
a. twenty churches
b. two cemeteries
c. numerous baths
d. a stadium
e. many mosaics

3.61 Any order:
a. the agora, or market place of the city
b. a theater
c. the temple of Apollo
d. many public buildings
e. private dwellings
f. pieces of pottery and other small objects
g. numerous inscriptions

3.62 Diana was the Asian goddess of fertility.

I. SECTION ONE

1.1 false

1.2 true

1.3 true

1.4 false

1.5 true

1.6 true

1.7 true

1.8 true

1.9 a body or system of teachings relating to a particular subject

1.10 doctrine of the Bible

1.11 God's disclosure of Himself and His will to His creatures

1.12 Any order:
   a. Aramaic
   b. Hebrew
   c. Greek

1.13 Either order:

   a. Natural revelation
   b. Specific revelation

1.14 Any order:

   a. Natural revelation is universal, that is, available to all human beings.
   b. Natural revelation is perfect since the Creator is perfect
   c. Natural revelation reveals God' eternal creative power and sovereignty.
   d. Natural revelation brings human beings to an awareness of God.
   e. Natural revelation cannot correct or overcome the blindness and unbelief intrinsic to the "fallen" human nature into which all human beings are born.

1.15 For this cause also thank we God without ceasing, because, when ye received the word of God which ye heard of us, ye received it not as the word of men, but as it is in truth, the word of God, which effectually worketh also in you that believe.

1.16 specific

1.17 Either order: written and living

1.18 Jesus, the Christ; the Bible

1.19 Either order: personal and direct

1.20 supernatural

1.21 the Bible

1.22 Christophany

1.23 theophany

1.24 Natural revelation reveals that God exists, that He is sovereign and powerful and can, through human conscience, convict people when doing harm and wrong, and cause them to long for justice and truth.

1.25 Specific revelation affords people the blessed privilege of knowing God and knowing Him as their creator God, their Savior God, and through Jesus, as their Heavenly Father. In specific revelation, God shows people their need and introduces His Christ, Jesus, as their savior and champion. In specific revelation, God lets people know how trusting in the person of Jesus and believing in the work of Jesus changes their position and their destiny immediately and for all eternity.

1.26 Study to shew thyself approved unto God, a workman that needeth not to be ashamed, rightly dividing the word of truth.

1.27 false

1.28 true

1.29 true

1.30 false

1.31 true

1.32   God-breathed

1.33   verbal

1.34   plenary

1.35   infallible

1.36   inerrancy

1.37   "And God spake all these words, saying,"

1.38   "Then said the LORD unto me, Thou hast well seen: for I will hasten my word to perform it"

1.39

	Christ's Incarnation	**Bible's Inspiration**
Initiated by	God	God
Human agency	Mary	Authors
Holy Spirit	Divine conception	Divine inspiration
Outcome	Sinless Savior	Inerrant Word

1.40   c

1.41   e

1.42   d

1.43   b

1.44   a

1.45   God's sovereign work that allows human beings to learn from divine revelation and to recognize divine truth.

1.46   Any order:
a.   The fall into sin by the parents of all human beings, Adam and Eve, has given us all a nature subject to sin and spiritual blindness
b.   Satan exploits our spiritual blindness so that he can keep people from the truth
c.   Only God the Holy Spirit brings light to all of God's truth that is necessary for one to know

1.47   true

1.48   false

1.49   true

1.50   true

1.51   false

1.52   A passage may have many applications, but it will have only one accurate interpretation. The aim and task of the interpreter is to discover that one, accurate interpretation and then apply it appropriately.

1.53   Any order:
a.   keep in mind the central message of the whole Bible and God' purpose with specific revelation
b.   gain understanding of the individual writers and their individual books
c.   place the passage in its proper historical setting
or   compare Scripture with Scripture

1.54   unnecessary

1.55   Either order:
a.   freedom
b.   blessing

1.56   The Scriptures

1.57   a.   God
b.   Man

1.58   a.   court
b.   appeal

1.59   "The scripture cannot be broken"

1.60   Any order:
a.   doctrine
b.   correction
c.   reproof
d.   instruction in righteousness

II. SECTION TWO

2.1   five thousand

2.2   oral tradition

2.3   patriarchs

2.4   430

2.5   nation

2.6   c

2.7   d

2.8   e

2.9   f

2.10   a

2.11   b

2.12   A nation needs written laws which can confirm and corroborate oral testimony, and to which subsequent generations can refer for adjudication of legal questions. A nation needs its Torah, Book of Law, to regulate its society and to preserve its freedoms.

2.13   Sheets and scrolls of papyrus had been invented as writing material, ink and simple pens had been created, phonograms had given way to alphabets, writing had now become accessible to people generally and practical for the communication of facts and ideas and for their preservation.

2.14   true

2.15   true

2.16   false

2.17   true

2.18   true

2.19   false

2.20   true

2.21   c

2.22   e

2.23   f

2.24   d

2.25   d

2.26   b

2.27   Former Prophets

2.28   Either order:
a. the Major Prophets
b. the Minor Prophets

2.29   a. the poetical books
b. the five rolls
c. the historical books

2.30   Any order:
a. What was the message to the original readership or audience?
b. What does this message teach with respect to the Messiah's advent---- his first coming as a babe in a manger?
c. What does this message show us with respect to Christ's second coming as returning, ruling King?

2.31   About 250 B.C., the Jewish community in Alexandria, Egypt, commissioned seventy scholars to translate the Hebrew Scriptures into Greek. This translation was called the Septuagint because 70 men worked on it. This Work restored the Holy Scriptures to a place of authority and influence in the Jewish community because they could be read and taught in Greek to people for whom Greek was their principal language. Greek, unlike Hebrew, includes characters for vowels and words and text includes characters for both; therefore, the Greek text required much more space on the page and necessitated dividing several scrolls into two books. Also the basic divisions used by the Hebrew Scriptures were expanded from three divisions to four: Law, Prophets, Writings and Poetical books

2.32   true

2.33   true

2.34   false

2.35   true

2.36   false

2.37   true

2.38   false

2.39   true

2.40   false

2.41   true

2.42   a. Matthew
       b. Mark
       c. Luke
       d. John

2.43   Any order:
       a. John
       b. Peter
       c. Matthew

2.44   Any order:
       a. Paul
       b. Apollos
       c. Sylvanus (Silas)

2.45   Any order:
       a. James
       b. Matthew
       c. Hebrews

2.46   unite

III. SECTION THREE

3.1   true

3.2   true

3.3   false

3.4   true

3.5   false

3.6   false

3.7   true

3.8   false

3.9   true

3.10   false

3.11   Any order:
       a. Were the books recognized, immediately, and also later, as being inspired by God?
       b. Were the books received by God's people, initially as well as later, as Holy Scripture?
       c. Were the books regularly preserved and collected by God's people?

3.12   a. Were the authors prophets, that is, did each author serve in the office of prophet; and/or did the author possess the spiritual gift of prophecy?
       b. Were the writings historically and prophetically accurate?

3.13   Messianic

3.14   Habakkuk

3.15   a. Internal claims to divine inspiration had to be compared with such claims in other canonical writings.
       b. References or quotes from the writing appearing in other canonical books had to be noted and verified.
       c. God's people must have accepted the writing as God's word and acted upon it as such.

3.16   Septuagint

3.17   Pseudepigrapha

3.18   Vulgate

3.19   Roman Catholic and Greek Orthodox

3.20   Either order:
       a. no canonical authors or books include any citations or quotations from any of these writings
       b. doctrines that are inconsistent with or contradictory to that taught in the canon are put forward in the Apocryphal writings.

3.21   Lord; pass; spoken; afraid

3.22   false

3.23   true

3.24   false

3.25   true

3.26   true

3.27   Clement

3.28   Diocletian

3.29   Constantine

3.30   Eusebius

3.31   Laodicea

3.32   Either order:
    a. Re-examinations of certain books or questions in light of archeological discoveries of ancient texts
    b. Cynicism, skepticism and unbelief of people who are anti-Christianity, anti-Christ and anti-God

1.1   a. Ruth and Naomi, faithfulness, loyalty
     b. David and Abiathar, protection
     c. David and Hanun, kindness, comfort
     d. David and Hiram, love, help
     e. **David and Jonathan (Mephibosheth), kindness, provisions, care**
     f. David and Hushai, risked his life
     g. David and Ittai, loyalty

1.2   e

1.3   b

1.4   a

1.5   f

1.6   d

1.7   false

1.8   true

1.9   true

1.10   true

1.11   false

1.12   commands

1.13   Scriptures

1.14   love

1.15   Either order:
     a. discipleship
     b. friendship or maturity

1.16   1 Corinthians chapter 13

1.17   He asked, "Who is my neighbor?"

1.18   **The lawyer answered, he that shewed (showed) mercy on him.**

1.19   The context of the Christian home is love, but the context of the world is hatred.

1.20   Example:
"He doth execute the judgment of the fatherless and widows, and loveth the stranger, in giving him food and raiment."

1.21   ". . . Inasmuch as ye have done it unto one of the least of these my brethren, ye have done it to me."

1.22   d. a, b, and c

1.23   c. a Samaritan

1.24   a. the home

1.25   d. a, b, and c

1.26   c. those at the king's right hand

1.27   Any order:
     a. hunger
     b. thirst
     c. stranger
     d. naked
     e. sick
     f. imprisoned

1.28   a. to pervert judgment
     b. to withold food

1.29   one who shows mercy

1.30   Examples:
     a. Nicodemus, a Pharisee, a ruler of the Jews, a master in Israel
     b. woman of Samaria, non-Jewish, worshiped in the mountain, adulteress
     c. leper, outcast, unclean
     d. rich young ruler, very religious, very rich, a ruler
     e. Matthew, a Levite, a publican
     f. Roman centurion, Gentile, occupational army
     g. woman of Canaan, Gentile, great faith
     h. Simon, Pharisee, religious
     i. woman taken in adultery, outcast
     j. one of the malefactors on the cross, not religious, outcast

1.31   d. both a and b

1.32   c. publicans

1.33   d. a, b, and c

1.34   d. a, b, and c

1.35   d. refuse him

1.36   Example:
The believer must seek out those that need him to help and those that he needs so he can grow.

1.37   Example:
The Scriptures teach that the needy, miserable, outcasts, sinners, saints, and those who need a friend are the ones we are to befriend.

1.38   Example:
The Scriptures tell us not to seek the company of the ungodly, sinners, and scornful.

1.39   Example:
Paul says that evil communication will corrupt good manners.

1.40   Example:
". . . why eateth your master with publicans and sinners?"

1.41   teacher check

II. SECTION TWO

2.1   d

2.2   b

2.3   a

2.4   e

2.5   c

2.6   The marriage arrangement of Isaac and Rebekah is described in Genesis 24:1-67.

2.7   Abraham sent his servant to choose a wife for Issac from Abraham's kindred.

2.8   Dating that practices Christian principles is scriptural.

2.9   The Scriptures teach us principles by which to live in our relationship to the opposite sex.

2.10   Example:
This scriptural admonition is given so that we might prove what is that good and acceptable and perfect will of God.

2.11   the practice or instance of having social engagements with a person of the opposite sex

2.12   Any order:
a. a relationship to the opposite sex
b. an expression of masculine initiative
c. a prearranged agreement
d. a parental consent and blessing
e. **a participation in a social engagement**
f. **a thoughtful and considered plan**

2.13   If one can establish and maintain a friendship with those of his own sex he can apply the same principles to the opposite sex.

2.14   leadership

2.15   **personal acquaintance, opportunity** for questions to be both answered and asked, expression of genuine interest and responsibility

2.16   teacher check

2.17   false

2.18   true

2.19   false

2.20   true

2.21   true

2.22   rudder

2.23   accepted of Him

2.24   pleased not Himself

2.25   the lusts of the flesh

2.26   new personal relationship

2.27   d. neither a, b, nor c

2.28   d. a, b, and c

2.29   d. a, b, and c

2.30   c. his sister

2.31   a. they need God's help

2.32   friendship

2.33   unteachable

2.34   looking realistically at dating

2.35   and the younger women as sisters, with all purity

2.36   the world

2.37   c

2.38   f

2.39   a

2.40   b

2.41   d

2.42   Either order:
       a. positive testimony of separation
       b. preparation for marriage

2.43   be holy (separate from the world) in every aspect of your life

2.44   Any order:
       a. please the Lord
       b. blessing to others
       c. testimony to unsaved

2.45   The change of relationship, from dating to marriage, does not change the principles of life.

III. SECTION THREE

3.1   Examples:
       Looking at the human race, God sees marriage as a necessity. Looking at the individual, God sees marriage as natural but not necessary.

3.2   God's Word is the only absolute authority on marriage.

3.3   Man's relationship to God, to woman, and to himself (unbelief, blame, guilt) were corrupted by the Fall.

3.4   Example:
       Only as man becomes a new creature and accepts God's purpose and principles for marriage can marriage honor the Lord.

3.5   Jesus added this note of authority to the Old Testament statement about marriage: ". . . what therefore God hath joined together, let not man put asunder."

3.6   false

3.7   true

3.8   true

3.9   true

3.10   false

3.11   neither marry nor are given in marriage

3.12   she is loosed from the law of her husband

3.13   they shall be one flesh

3.14   a physical aspect to it

3.15   the laws and principles recorded in the Scriptures

3.16   eternal significance

3.17   a physical side

3.18   she be married to another man

3.19   part of the foundation of society

3.20   put to death

3.21   c

3.22   g

3.23   a or f

3.24   f

3.25   b

3.26　d

3.27　e

3.28　a. marriage covenant
　　　b. death terminates the marriage union
　　　c. one flesh
　　　d. no marriage relationship in heaven

3.29　Answer should include:
near of kin, father's wife, sister, granddaughter, half sister, father's sister (aunt), mother's sister, father's brother's wife, daughter-in-law, sister-in-law, mother and daughter, sister, neighbor's wife

3.30　a. holiness in marriage
　　　b. holiness in mixed marriages
　　　c. church leadership
　　　d. family and community influence
　　　e. heirs of the gift of life

3.31　Either order:
　　　a. husband's love
　　　b. wife's subjection

3.32　false

3.33　true

3.34　true

3.35　false

3.36　true

3.37　be fruitful, multiply, replenish the earth and subdue it

3.38　Examples:
deep personal friendship, companionship, sharpen personality, meet social needs, provide family context for rearing children, provide experienced leadership for church and community

3.39　No, the purpose does not change

3.40　d

3.41　a

3.42　f

3.43　b

3.44　c

3.45　d. a, b, and c

3.46　d. a, b, and c

3.47　d. a, b, and c

3.48　c. wisdom of God

3.49　a. Ephesians chapter 5

3.50　b

3.51　a

3.52　b

3.53　b

3.54　a

3.55　Any order:
　　　a. Church subject to Christ; wives submit unto husbands
　　　b. Christ head of the Church: husband head of the wife
　　　c. Christ loved the Church; husbands love wives
　　　d. Christ nourish and cherish Church; husband nourish and cherish wife

Section I

1.1 Bathsheba, David

1.2 Absalom

1.3 Adonijah

1.4 Nathan

1.5 Abiathar

1.6 Nathan, Zadok

1.7 horns

1.8 Shimei

1.9 Abiathar

1.10 40

1.11 6

1.12 Adonijah, Bathsheba

1.13 970

1.14 David

1.15 Joab

1.16 Barzillai

1.17 Jesus or Christ

Section II

2.1 wisdom

2.2 seven

2.3 fire

2.4 tabernacle

2.5 David

2.6 Moriah

2.7 two

2.8 King Hiram or Tyre

2.9 idol

2.10 gold

2.11 o

2.12 a

2.13 f

2.14 b

2.15 k

2.16 l

2.17 c

2.18 i

2.19 d

2.20 j

2.21 m

2.22 p

2.23 e

2.24 g

2.25 h

2.26 q

2.27 n

2.28 false

2.29 true

2.30 true

2.31 false

2.32 true

2.33 diplomacy

2.34 taxed

2.35 Queen of Sheba

2.36 idols or foreign gods

2.37 King Hiram

2.38 masters

2.39 Abraham

2.40 Egypt

2.41 throne

2.42 world

2.43 Suggested answers:

Command	Disobedience
• do not multiply horses or return to Egypt for horses	• Solomon had 40,000 horses and imported horses from Egypt
• do not multiply wives for yourself	• he had 700 wives and princesses and 300 concubines
• do not greatly increase silver or gold for yourself	• 666 talents of gold came in each year; he made 500 shields of gold; all his drinking vessels were gold
• fear God and carefully observe all the words of His law	• he worshipped the idols of his wives; built high places for idol worship and sacrificed to idols

Section III

3.1 He is referred to as Elohim, the all-powerful creator.

3.2 It begins with a secular theme—meaningless that resulted in living apart from God.

3.3 Suggested answers:

Against: The title Quoheleth can be translated to mean wisdom teacher or leader of the assembly, which could possibly refer to a leader other than Solomon. Some scholars find it odd that a book written by Solomon makes no mention of his building projects or kingdom expansion. Scholars also believe that the writing style in Ecclesiastes better matches the writing style of Malachi, the Old Testament book, which would place the writing of Ecclesiastes at a much later date than Solomon.

For: The author introduced himself as Israel's king reigning in Jerusalem. Only three kings reigned over the united kingdom of Israel from Jerusalem: David, Solomon, and, briefly, Rehoboam. Ecclesiastes has been, throughout history, firmly linked with Solomon, whose experiences fit the theme of the book.

3.4 The book of Ecclesiastes was read every year at the Feast of Tabernacles (also called the Feast of Booths), the first significant holiday of the new year.

3.5 false

3.6 false

3.7 true

3.8 true

3.9 false

3.10 true

3.11 true

3.12 false

3.13 false

3.14 false

3.15 false

3.16 true

3.17 true

3.18 false

3.19 true

3.20 false

3.21 true

3.22 true

I SECTION ONE

1.1 a. Atheist
    b. Agnostic
    c. Infidel
    d. Skeptic
    e. Critical
    f. Inquirer

1.2 should not ignore them, but rather try to understand them and clear up the misunderstanding

1.3 Example:
    Trust God's Word; examine problem passages, either reach a conclusion or suspend judgment

1.4 c

1.5 f

1.6 a

1.7 g

1.8 e

1.9 b

1.10 Any order:
    a. doctrinal variances
    b. ethical variances
    c. numerical variances
    d. factual variances
    e. parallel passages

1.11 Any order:
    a. figures of speech or visual imagery:
    Many Biblical writers chose to describe nature in poetic form rather than technical language.

    b. human viewpoints:
    We have a tendency to describe natural occurrences from our own perspective, or point of observation.

    c. improper translations:
    Some words in Scripture, such as names of animals, are not properly translated from the original language into English.

1.12 a. Psalm 139:14
    b. Job 14:9
    c. Ecclesiastes 1:6-7
    d. Job 38:31
    e. Hebrews 11:3
    f. Leviticus 17:11
    g. Matthew 6:28-29
    h. Job 39:29
    i. Proverbs 17:22
    j. Deuteronomy 14:21

II SECTION TWO

2.1 Any order:
    a. "All religions contain some truth."
    b. "All roads lead to Rome."
    c. "Good, sincere people are in all religions."

2.2 Any order:
    a. It follows the authentic Word of God, not the teachings of men.
    b. Its God is a Trinity, not a simple deity.
    c. It has a resurrected Saviour, not a dead founder.
    d. It offers salvation by grace, not works.

2.3 teacher check

2.4 Either order:
    a. intuition: The innate need of man to worship someone or something bears evidence of God's existence.
    b. personal experience: Our new birth and our individual spiritual experiences verify God's presence in us.

2.5 c

2.6 a

2.7 b

2.8 Any order:
    a. performed by God or His agents
    b. unique, special acts
    c. objective, verified occurrences
    d. purposeful

2.9 a. supersedure
     b. timing
     c. intervention
     Examples:
2.10 a-b Either order:
     a. omnipotence
     b. eternal existence
     c-d Either order:
     c. creation
     d. forgiveness

2.11 The Lord created the world and
     mankind for His own pleasure, for
     fellowship, and for His glory.

2.12 Any order:
     a. power
     b. patience
     c. justice
     d. holiness
     e. grace
     f. love

2.13 true

2.14 true

2.15 false

2.16 true

2.17 false

2.18 a. Nature reveals God.
     b. Men rejected God when they
         knew Him.
     c. Men prefer sin to God.
     Example:
2.19 Jesus loved, admired, and respected
     children, and He urged others to
     follow a child's example of
     simplicity and faith.
     Example:
2.20 the age at which a child knows
     and understands who Jesus is and
     becomes accountable for his sins
     and for his decision to accept
     or reject Christ

2.21 a. earth's atmosphere
     b. realm of planets and stars
     c. third heaven, God's abode

2.22 false

2.23 false

2.24 true

2.25 true

2.26 false

2.27 true

III SECTION THREE

3.1 a. It is inconsistent to accept
         some parts of the biblical
         account and not others.
     b. Noah would not have needed it
         because he could have migrated
         to an unflooded area.
     c. He promised never to destroy
         the earth again with a flood.
     d. All men have descended from
         Noah's three sons.

3.2 Any order:
     a. Universal adjectives describe it.
     b. It covered all mountain peaks.
     c. It lasted over a year.
3.3 Any order:
     a. Their formation requires
         sudden burial.
     b. It shows evidence that it was deposited
         during the various stages of a massive
         flood.

     c. Its irregularities show
         evidence of flooding.
3.4 a. Ararat
     b. Turkey

3.5 sightings

3.6 Genesis 6:15-16

3.7 ice

3.8 Bible

3.9 true

3.10 true

3.11 true

3.12 false

3.13 false

3.14 We would probably not be so watchful
     and prayerful and most likely
     would delay our spiritual preparation.

3.15 Either order:
a. believing the promises of God
b. the witness of the Holy Spirit

3.16 Those promises which make the
prayers of God's people a condition
for their fulfillment.

3.17 Any order:
a. saving
b. **believing**
c. yielding
d. obeying
e. continuing

3.18 Israel

3.19 keep

3.20 grace

3.21 Holy Spirit

3.22 a. outward
b. inward

3.23 Sabbath

3.24 false

3.25 true

3.26 false

3.27 false

3.28 true

3.29 true

3.30 Either order:
a. The Bible assures us of the
ultimate triumph of justice.
b. The Bible assures us of God's
purpose for suffering.

3.31 Any order:
a. to correct our sin
b. to teach obedience
c. to turn from sin
d. to cause us to mature
spiritually
e. to learn to depend upon God
or glorify God

BIBLE 1110

I. SECTION ONE

1.1 false

1.2 false

1.3 false

1.4 true

1.5 true

1.6 Either order:
a. natural
b. specific

1.7 a. holiness
b. sinfulness

1.8 awareness

1.9 Any order:
a. nature
b. man's conscience
c. God's Word, the Bible

1.10 Either order:
a. Romans 1:20
b. Psalm 19:1

1.11 Example:
to communicate to man things about Himself that would otherwise be unknown; to "unveil" Himself to man

1.12 d

1.13 f

1.14 g

1.15 a

1.16 c

1.17 e

1.18 Example:
to allow man to have a personal relationship with Him through Jesus Christ who was the culmination of all the specific revelations

1.19 true

1.20 true

1.21 true

1.22 false

1.23 Peter

1.24 God-breathed

1.25 a. dictate
b. control

1.26 isogogics

1.27 Christians

1.28 Any order:
a. A passage may have many applications but only one interpretation.
b. All passages should be studied in their context.
c. Introductory studies, or isogogics, must be done.

1.29 Example:
Second Timothy 3:16 reminds us that the Word of God is profitable to the Christian in all areas of life.

1.30 true

1.31 false

1.32 false

1.33 false

1.34 true

1.35 pictographic

1.36 orally

1.37 Examples; either order:
a. God waited until man had reached a point where he could easily record God's Word in written form.
b. He waited until Israel had emerged as a nation and needed laws to guarantee their individual freedom and demonstrate national freedoms.

1.38 k

1.39 a

1.40 g

1.41 c

1.42 d

1.43 e

1.44 f

1.45 h

1.46 i

1.47 **b**

1.48 Any order:
a. The Torah
b. The Prophets
c. The Writings

1.49 Any order:
a. Joshua
b. Judges
c. Samuel
d. Kings

1.50 true

1.51 false

1.52 true

1.53 false

1.54 false

1.55 true

1.56 Moses

1.57 Malachi

1.58 Megilloth

1.59 Writings

1.60 Example:
There was more room required to accomodate the Greek language. Greek contains vowels while the Hebrew language does not. More room was needed for the Greek. Thus they added another section.

1.61-1.63 Examples:
1.61 the recognition of God's revelation to man

1.62 a Greek word that refers to a reed that was used as a measuring rod

1.63 reliability; genuineness

1.64 true

1.65 true

1.66 false

1.67 false

1.68 a. A.D. 100-150
b. Epistles
c. Apologists
d. New Testament
e. 300-590
f. Laodicea

1.69 Any order:
a. Is it prophetic?
b. Is it dynamic?
c. Is it authoritative?
or Is it authentic?
Was it received by God's people?

1.70 Any order:
a. Did the text claim inspiration?
b. Was the text apostolic in origin?
c. Was the book consistent with other inspired works?
d. Was the work recognized as being from God? or Did the writing contain exhortation for public use? or Was the book received by the churches?

1.71 Example:
Certain doctrinal differences with the Scriptures made them unacceptable. II Maccabees mentions prayers being made on behalf of saints who have died.

1.72 The Age of Theologians

1.73 Resurrection

1.74 Prophets

1.75 Babylonian Exile

1.76 Either order:
a. Psuedepigrapha
b. Aprocrypha

1.77 Mari Tablets

1.78 Dead Sea Scrolls

1.79 Rosetta Stone

1.80 Nuzi

1.81 1947

1.82 Khirbet Qumran

1.83 a. ancient
b. culture or life

1.84 Teacher check—Optional:
The discovery of the Ebla Tablets showed the existence of such Biblical names as Daniel and Abraham. The Tablets provided further insight to the nature of the area in the Middle East around 2500 B.C.

II. SECTION TWO

2.1 d

2.2 c

2.3 e

2.4 b

2.5 Day of Pentecost

2.6 Either order:
a. pantheism or Judaism
b. deification

2.7 Any order:
a. senatorial aristocracy
b. equestrian order
c. freedmen
d. plebes

2.8 Either order:
a. to establish fundamental doctrines and to fortify the Romans against the influence of the Judaizers
b. to urge the Romans to maturity
or to reveal to the Romans their relationship to each other and the government and the relationships between Jews and Gentiles in the church
or to explain the unbelief of Israel
or to send personal greetings

2.9 a. Romans 1:16-17
b. "For I am not ashamed of the gospel of Christ: for it is the power of God unto salvation to everyone that believeth; to the Jew first, and also to the Greek. For therein is the righteousness of God revealed from faith to faith: as it is written, The just shall live by faith."

2.10 a. thanksgiving
b. downward spiral of sin
c. 2-3
d. Abraham
e. Justification
f. justification
g. baptism
h. Carnal
i. spiritual
j. Holy Spirit

2.11 to miss the mark

2.12 faith

2.13 Any order:
a. inheritance
b. righteousness
c. posterity

2.14 Habbakuk 2:4

2.15 Romans 5:1 "Therefore being justified by faith, we have peace with God through our Lord Jesus Christ." Romans 5:8 "But God commendeth his love toward us, in that, while we were yet sinners, Christ died for us."

2.16 true

2.17 true

2.18 false

2.19 true

2.20 teacher check:
Check to see if student can effectively use the verses to reveal God's plan of salvation. Knowing these verses is a key to successful witnessing.

2.21 a. sovereignty
b. Jewish
c. Gentiles
d. service
e. submission
f. conscience
g. consideration

2.22 Any order:
a. adoption
b. glory
c. covenants
d. giving of the Law
e. service of God
f. promises
g. the fathers
h. lineage leading to Christ

2.23 Either order:
a. Jew
b. Greek (Gentile)

2.24 a. ignorant
b. righteousness

2.25 Any order:
a. How then shall they call on him in whom they have not believed?
b. How shall they believe in him of whom they have not heard?
c. How shall they hear without a preacher?
d. How shall they preach, except they be sent?

2.26 true

2.27 false

2.28 true

2.29 false

2.30 false

2.31 true

2.32 true

2.33 Example:
God has established all human governments and uses them to work for the good of His people.

2.34 Example:
We are separated from its values, ways, and goals. We should not adopt its ways.

2.35 Example:
so that the plan of salvation and redemption of the Gentiles through Jesus Christ would be open

2.36 Hosea and Isaiah

2.37 teacher check

III. SECTION THREE

3.1 a binding or solemn agreement made by two or more parties

3.2 d

3.3 d

3.4 c

3.5 d

3.6 false

3.7 false

3.8 true

3.9 true

3.10 true

3.11 Example:
Five animals (except the birds) were cut in two and while Abraham slept. A smoking furnace and a burning lamp passed between the pieces.

3.12 400

3.13 Any order:
a. Persian
b. Greek
c. Roman

3.14 Either order:
a. Ptolemies
b. Seleucids

3.15 a. eight
b. 25

3.16 Example:
The persecution of Jews, destruction
of copies of Scriptures, attempts
to destroy the Jewish faith by
the Syrian ruler, Antiochus
Epiphanes.

3.17 Example:
a militant Jewish faction

3.18 Example:
in protest of the building of
the Roman city Aelia Capitolina
in Jerusalem

3.19 ". . . until the fullness of the
Gentiles be come in."

3.20 resiliency

3.21 1948

3.22 discrimination

3.23 **Moslems**

3.24 People's Crusade

3.25 eighteenth

3.26 true

3.27 true

3.28 false

3.29 true

3.30 true

3.31 Example:
Abraham may be viewed as God, the
Father who initiated the Covenant
and was willing to sacrifice His
son. Isaac may be viewed as Jesus
and Jacob may be viewed as the
Holy Spirit who multiplied himself

3.32 Example:
the Scriptures; heritage of God's
faithfulness; Jesus, the Saviour;
examples of faith demonstrated by
the lives of the Old Testament
patriarchs

3.33 Teacher check; example:
In the general sense, no, but overall they have not recognized Christ
as Saviour. Their faithfulness to
God does not seem to show through
to the rest of the world. The
existence of Israel, however, as
a state, is an example of God's
faithfulness.

IV. SECTION FOUR

4.1 true

4.2 false

4.3 true

4.4 Example:
God is able to supply all our
physical, mental, and spiritual
needs. God is the Shepherd of mankind.

4.5 teacher check

4.6 **Example:**
that God is pitiful and merciful

4.7 teacher check

4.8 Example:
That God is faithful to man even
under difficult circumstances.
Everything that happens to us will
not be understood. God is working
to help us trust Him in the difficult
circumstances that do arise.

4.9 Any order:
a. pleasure
b. money
c. power
d. sex
or reputation, prestige

4.10 covenants

4.11 true

4.12 true

4.13 Example:
One of the Old Testament prophets, the resurrected John the Baptist, Elijah or Jeremiah

4.14 Son of the living God

4.15 Any order:
a. charismatic leader
b. social activist
c. political revolutionary
or religious leader or just a great man

4.16 Either order:
a. He concealed the manifestation of His divine glory.
b. He limited the use of certain divine attributes.

4.17 Example:
He experienced a normal childhood, adolescence, and adulthood. He suffered temptations like we have. He was recognized as being Jewish.

4.18 Any order:
a. Son of God
b. God
c. Emmanuel
d. Word of God or Lord

4.19 Any order:
a. immutable
b. omnipresent
c. omnipotent
d. eternal

4.20 conveys the meaning of the future glory of God's kingdom and the man who represents the human race, who will execute judgment over mankind

4.21 God with us

4.22 Either order:
a. respect
b. esteem

4.23 Either order:
a. nature
b. character

4.24 a. fulness
b. Godhead

4.25 true

4.26 true

4.27 true

4.28 Any order:
a. made an atonement for man's sin
b. redeemed man—the penalty for sin was paid
c. reconciled man to God
or appeased God's holy anger against sin, as a substitute for sinners

4.29 Either order:
a. Priest
b. King

4.30 Any order:
a. swoon theory
b. hallucination theory
c. disciples stole the body
or Christ resurrected spiritually and not bodily

4.31 Any order:
a. Advocate
b. Mediator
c. Ambassador
or Intercessor, High Priest, Head of the body of Christ

4.32 death on the Cross

4.33 Resurrection

4.34 a. testimony
b. empty

V. SECTION FIVE

5.1 Any order:
a. faith
b. hope
c. love or charity

5.2 charity
or love

5.3 Example:
There is a need for certain personal relationships and love among other Christians.

5.4 Example:
They prove that love persists in spite of the cost. Their love was the highest form of love.

5.5 Example:
The intimate relationships found in the family will help shape and mold us to reach out to others with love, kindness, forgiveness, and encouragement.

5.6 Example:
We should select friends that are not sinners, scoffers, or would try to make us follow their ways.

5.7 a. planned
b. opposite

5.8 preparation

5.9 true

5.10 false

5.11 true

5.12 Either order:
a. Man and woman were to become one flesh.
b. The man would leave his father and mother and cleave to his wife.

5.13 Any order:
a. holiness
b. responsibility in bringing up children
c. contributions to the church and community

5.14 for man and woman to be fruitful, multiply and replenish the earth, and subdue it

5.15 Example:
The roles of the man and woman changed. God's purpose for marriage did not change, but it will now be done through suffering and sorrow.

5.16 false

5.17 true

5.18 false

5.19 Fear God and keep His commandments.

5.20 Example:
pursuing happiness apart from God will fail. These things (money, pleasure) will not fulfill the Christian apart from God's grace.

5.21 Example:
When he was a very old man and realized the fruitlessness of his search.

5.22 His relationship with Jesus Christ.

5.23 willingness

5.24 a. guarantee, or seal
b. sanctify

5.25 Example:
Christian apologetics is simply sharing your faith and the claims of Christ openly and honestly to someone who asks a reason for the hope that is in you. Apologetics should not be used to win an argument.

5.26 The Bible

5.27 "But sanctify the Lord God in your hearts: and be ready always to give an answer to every man that asketh you a reason of the hope that is in you with meekness and fear."

5.28 Optional; teacher check

5.29 false

5.30 true

5.31 true

5.32 Teacher check; example:
Jesus told the women that He was the living water and that He was the source of eternal life. He exposed, or convicted, her of her sin and told her that He was the Messiah and the way to God.

SELF TEST 1

1.01   true

1.02   true

1.03   false

1.04   true

1.05   false

1.06   true

1.07   true

1.08   true

1.09   true

1.010   false

1.011   false

1.012   Any order:
        a. I shall not want
        b. I will fear no evil
        c. I will dwell in the house of
           the LORD forever

1.013   e

1.014   h

1.015   j

1.016   m

1.017   k

1.018   a

1.019   b

1.020   n

1.021   o

1.022   g

1.023   c

1.024   i

1.025   f

1.026   d

1.027   l

1.028   His goodness and mercy shall fol-
        low me all the days of my life; I
        will dwell in the house of the
        LORD forever.

1.029   Example:
        "The Lord gave, and the Lord hath taken
        away; blessed be the name of the
        Lord." ... "shall we receive good at
        the hand of God and shall we
        not receive evil?

1.030   a. He saw God in a way he had not
           seen Him before.
        b. He abhorred (hated, despised)
           himself and repented.
        c. The LORD gave Job twice as much
           as he had before.
        d. He had seven sons and three
           daughters.
        e. After this Job lived 140 years.

1.031   "Nevertheless, my loving kindness
        will I not utterly take from him,
        nor suffer my faithfulness to fail.
        My covenant will I not break, nor
        alter the thing that is gone out
        of my lips. Once have I sworn by
        my holiness that I will not lie
        unto David."

1.032   "Behold, we count them happy which
        endure. Ye have heard of the pa-
        tience of Job, and have seen the
        end of the Lord; that the Lord is
        very pitiful, and of tender mercy."

1.033   "There shall not any man be able
        to stand before thee all the days
        of thy life: as I was with Moses,
        so I will be with thee: I will not
        fail thee, nor forsake thee. Be
        strong and of a good courage: for
        unto this people shalt thou divide
        for an inheritance the land, which
        I swore unto their father to give
        them."

SELF TEST 2

2.01   a. Rock
        b. Fixity or steadfastness

2.02 Examples:
perfect, absolute or never fails

2.03 Either order:
a. immutability
b. universality

2.04 Either order:
a. counsel
b. oath

2.05 God is faithful to all that He made.

2.06 "Thy faithfulness is unto all generations."

2.07 The seed of woman would bruise the head of the serpent – promise of a Redeemer.

2.08 a. Some believe.
b. Some do not believe.

2.09 He abideth faithful.

2.010 God causes the rain to fall on the just and the unjust

2.011 Either order:
a. God's Word
b. God's work

2.012 Example:
"An attribute of God, implying loyalty, constancy, and freedom from arbitrariness or fickleness."

2.013 Examples; any order:
a. Abideth faithful
b. Not suffer my faithfulness to fail
c. I have sworn
d. There hath not failed one word.
e. Keepeth truth forever

2.014 Examples; any order:
a. forgiveness of sins and iniquities
b. no condemnation to those in Christ
c. everlasting life for those who hear and believe
d. wisdom given liberally if we ask
e. answered prayer if in accord with His will
f. help in temptation; no unbearable temptation

g. peace will keep our heart through Christ Jesus
h. fruitfulness if we abide in Christ
i. no one can "pluck" us out of Christ
j. prepared place so we can be with Him

2.015 "Thy faithfulness is unto all generations: thou hast established the earth, and it abideth."

2.016 "God is not a man, that he should lie; neither the son of man, that he should repent: hath he said, and shall he not do it? or hath he spoken, and shall he not make it good?"

2.017 Any order:
a. The Lord gave and the Lord has taken away.
b. Shall we receive good at the hand of God and shall we not receive evil?
c. Though He slay me, yet will I trust Him.

2.018 The Lord blessed the latter end of Job more than his beginning.

SELF TEST 3

3.01 c

3.02 b

3.03 a

3.04 b

3.05 b

3.06 b

3.07 b

3.08 Any order:
a. Creator
b. witness
c. High Priest

3.09 Either order:
a. His providential care
b. His covenant with His creatures to restore them.

3.010 Any order:
a. uphold
b. direct
c. dispose
d. govern

3.011 God will establish David's throne forever.

3.012 Sinless, holy—only sacrifice for sin

3.013 Sinless, holy—only way to God

3.014 Perfect and absolute

3.015 Either order:
a. Immutability
b. Universality

3.016 God remains faithful

3.017 Psalm 23

3.018 Example:
His main concern was that the unity of the believers be kept while they were here on earth.

3.019 Example:
Faithfulness is an attribute of God implying loyalty, constancy, and freedom from arbitrariness or fickleness.

3.020 Example:
We can best learn of the faithfulness of God through His Word and His works.

3.021 Examples; any order:
a. I and the Father are one.
b. He that hath seen me hath seen the Father.
c. I in thee and thou in me.

3.022 Examples; any order:
a. Sinless priest
b. Never dies
c. Makes perfect
d. Never to be repeated
e. Based on better promises

3.023 Examples; any order:
a. My record is true.
b. My judgment is true.
c. He that sent me is true, and I speak those words which I have heard.

3.024 Examples; any order:
a. He makes us lie down in green pastures.
b. He restores our souls.
c. He leads us beside still waters.
d. He prepares a table for us in the presence of our enemies.

3.025 "Wherefore let them that suffer according to the will of God commit the keeping of their souls to Him in well doing, as unto a faithful creator."

3.026 "Wherefore in all things it behoved him to be made like unto his brethren, that he might be a merciful and faithful high priest in things pertaining to God, to make reconciliation for the sins of the people."

SELF TEST 4

4.01 Either order:
a. We have a moral and rational obligation to trust Him.
b. We are obliged to be faithful with what He entrusts to us.

4.02 a. Creator
b. High Priest
c. Witness

4.03 the Word

4.04 to be a steward of that grace

4.05 a. not an owner
b. must give an account, or faithfulness

4.06 Faithfulness is the fruit of the Holy Spirit.

4.07 yes

4.08 Christ will bring his reward with Him.

4.09   a. His Word
        b. His work

4.010   Shepherd

4.011   Any order:
        a. I shall not want.
        b. I will fear no evil.
        c. I will dwell in the house of
           the LORD forever.

4.012   perfect, absolute or never fails

4.013   unto all generations

4.014   b

4.015   c

4.016   a

4.017   c

4.018   a

4.019   d

4.020   e

4.021   b

4.022   Example:
        The unfaithful steward found out
        human cleverness is sometimes
        commendable, but it will not
        free one from the penalty for
        unfaithfulness.

4.023   Examples; either order:
        a. He will be rewarded for his
           own works.
        b. He will be rewarded for only
           those works that come through
           the fire.

4.024   Examples; any order:
        a. Persecution for Christ's sake
        b. Loving your enemies
        c. Preaching the gospel willingly
        d. Labor for earthly masters

4.025   Examples:
        a. Conditional-Mosaic Law
        b. Unconditional-Abrahamic Covenant

4.026   b

4.027   a

4.028   c

4.029   "Wherefore in all things it behoved
        him to be made like unto his breth-
        ren, that he might be a merciful
        and faithful high priest in things
        pertaining to God, to make recon-
        ciliation for the sins of the people."

4.030   "Wherefore let them that suffer
        according to the will of God commit
        the keeping of their souls to him
        in well doing, as unto a faithful
        Creator."

4.031   "And many other signs truly did
        Jesus in the presence of his
        disciples, which are not written
        in this book: But these are written
        that ye might believe that Jesus
        is the Christ, the Son of God; and
        that believing ye might have life
        through his name."

SELF TEST 1

1.01   f

1.02   d

1.03   e

1.04   h

1.05   i

1.06   a

1.07   b

1.08   j

1.09   c

1.010   g

1.011   a. Augustus
        b. Tiberius
        c. Caligula (Gaius)
        d. Claudius
        e. Nero

1.012   a. senatorial aristocracy
        b. equestrian order
        c. freedmen (emancipated slaves)
        d. plebes
        e. slaves

1.013   b. Spain

1.014   c. stola

1.015   d. taxes

1.016   d. A.D. 57-58

1.017   d. only for governmental business

1.018   a. Augustus

1.019   d. govern the provinces

1.020   b. available to all

1.021   c. the founding of a popular
           apostle

1.022   d. sin and God's solution for it

1.023   form

1.024   Jewish sect

1.025   agriculture

1.026   Greek

1.027   synagogues

1.028   Mediterranean Sea

1.029   circus

1.030   Praetorian Guard

1.031   Greeks

1.032   Claudius

1.033   Answer should include:
        It began its growth at Jerusalem on the
        Day of Pentecost. Some members were
        Paul's friends and converts. Once
        thrown out of synagogues, believers met
        in homes. The believers at Rome
        had no centralized organization.
        Leadership for each group was a
        decision made by the individual
        congregations. The worship
        consisted of singing psalms,
        exercising spiritual gifts, prayer,
        and the reading and exposition of
        the Scriptures. The rites of baptism
        and the Lord's Supper, or love feast,
        were a part of every Christian church.

SELF TEST 2

2.01   h

2.02   d

2.03   e

2.04   f

2.05   a

2.06   b

2.07   i

2.08   c

2.09   j

2.010   g

2.011   b

2.012   d

2.013 a

2.014 c

2.015 d

2.016 c

2.017 a

2.018 a

2.019 b

2.020 b

2.021 d

2.022 b

2.023 d

2.024 c

2.025 a

2.026 d

2.027 c

2.028 b

2.029 a

2.030 b

2.031 b

2.032 c

2.033 a

2.034 d

2.035 d

2.036 condemnation

2.037 good

2.038 conquerors

2.039 peace

2.040 separate

2.041 a. Augustus
b. Tiberius
c. Caligula (Gaius)
d. Claudius
e. Nero

2.042 check with page 19

2.043 "For I am not ashamed of the
gospel of Christ: for it is the
power of God unto salvation to
everyone that believeth; to the
Jew first, and also to the Greek.
For therein is the righteousness
of God revealed from faith to
faith: as it is written, The
just shall live by faith."
(Romans 1:16-17)

2.044 Jewish proselytes were the only ones
who could become Christians. Only
the circumcised could be heirs
to the promises of God. Paul explained circumcision as being a
token of faith to be counted as
righteousness, not as a means for
righteousness.

2.045 The Law brings knowledge of right
and wrong. Sin deceives men into
believing that the Law separates
them from happiness. Once man acts
on the deception by breaking the
Law, the Law becomes a means by
which a person can be judged and
condemned.

2.046 teacher check

SELF TEST 3

3.01 f

3.02 i

3.03 n

3.04 b

3.05 m

3.06 o

3.07 a

3.08 k

3.09   c

3.010   h

3.011   j

3.012   g

3.013   d

3.014   l

3.015   e

3.016   false

3.017   true

3.018   true

3.019   true

3.020   false

3.021   true

3.022   false

3.023   false

3.024   true

3.025   true

3.026   Adam

3.027   sin

3.028   Word of God

3.029   nature

3.030   justification by faith in Jesus Christ

3.031   death

3.032   eternal

3.033   love

3.034   Nicodemus

3.035   blood

3.036   death

3.037   Holy Spirit

3.038   c. Greek

3.039   d. anyone

3.040   b. the Jews

3.041   c. only for governmental business

3.042   b. an apostle

3.043   a. reprobate or b. autonomous

3.044   c. Adam

3.045   a. the infallible Word of God

3.046   d. believes in the atoning
        work of Jesus' blood

3.047   b. a single event

3.048   a. Augustus
        b. Tiberius
        c. Caligula (Gaius)
        d. Claudius
        e. Nero

3.049   Any order:
        a. senatorial aristocracy
        b. equestrian order
        c. freedmen
        d. plebes
        e. slaves

3.050   Any five; any order:
        a. protect them from Judaizers
        b. establish them in fundamental
           doctrine
        c. secure support for work in Spain
        d. explain unbelief of Israel
        e. urge participation in body of
           Christ
        f. maintain unity by submitting to
           authority
        g. send greetings
        h. commend Phoebe
        i. introduce himself

3.051   "For I am not ashamed of the gospel
        of Christ: for it is the power of
        God unto salvation to everyone that
        believeth; to the Jew first, and also
        to the Greek. For therein is the
        righteousness of God revealed from
        faith to faith: as it is written,
        The just shall live by faith."

3.052 "For all have sinned and come short of the glory of God."

3.053 "For the wages of sin is death; but the gift of God is eternal life through Jesus Christ our Lord."

3.054 "Therefore being justified by faith, we have peace with God through our Lord Jesus Christ."

3.055 "But God commendeth his love toward us, in that, while we were yet sinners, Christ died for us."

3.056 "Likewise reckon ye also yourselves dead indeed to sin, but alive unto God through Jesus Christ our Lord."

3.057 "Therefore there is now no condemnation to them which are in Christ Jesus, who walk not after the flesh, but after the Spirit."

3.058 "Romans 1:1-17—Salutation
Romans 1:18-2:29—Downward spiral of sin
Romans 3—Universal sin and guilt, with emphasis on the Jewish nation
Romans 4—Abraham
Romans 5—Justification
Romans 6—Reckoning justification by baptism
Romans 7—Carnal nature vs. Spiritual nature
Romans 8—Life in the Holy Spirit

SELF TEST 1

1.01 d

1.02 g

1.03 j

1.04 f

1.05 a

1.06 i

1.07 c

1.08 b

1.09 h

1.010 e

1.011 true

1.012 true

1.013 true

1.014 false

1.015 true

1.016 false

1.017 false

1.018 true

1.019 a. Jewish rejection and unbelief

1.020 c. the ministry of reconciliation

1.021 b. to be adopted and accepted in the beloved

1.022 d. Jeremiah

1.023 c. hearing

1.024 c. the Gentiles

1.025 a. the Law

1.026 d. 1-2

1.027 c. circumcision

1.028 d. Jewish unbelief

1.029 knowledge

1.030 olive tree

1.031 "home churches"

1.032 wild olive branch

1.033 be highminded, but fear; don't boast against the Jews

1.034 Any order:
a. the glory
b. the covenants
c. the giving of the law
d. the service of God
e. the adoption (sonship)
   OR
   the promises
   the patriarchal heritage
   the Messiah

1.035 Example:
God's sovereignty should invoke a response of worship and reverential awe from those of use who know and love him, rather than visualizing a cruel God who wants to send us all to hell.

1.036 Example:
Paul had made the statement that anyone who called on the name of the Lord would be saved, but explained that before a person could call on the name of the Lord they must first believe that Jesus died for their sin, was buried, and rose again. Secondly, they must hear the Gospel for "faith come by hearing and by the word of God." Thirdly, a preacher must verbally relate the message of salvation. Fourthly, the preacher must be sent by God. It is the responsibility of every Christian to go forth with the good news of Jesus Christ.

1.037
a. Romans 1:1-1:17 Salutation
b. Romans 1:18-2:29 Downward spiral of sin
c. Romans 3 Universal sin and guilt, with emphasis on the Jews
d. Romans 4 Abraham
e. Romans 5 Justification
f. Romans 6 Reckoning justification by baptism
g. Roman 7 Carnal nature vs. spiritual nature
h. Romans 8 Life in the Holy Spirit
i. Romans 9 God's sovereignty
j. Romans 10 Jewish unbelief
k. Romans 11 Grafting of the Gentiles

SELF TEST 2

2.01 m

2.02 d

2.03 j

2.04 l

2.05 h

2.06 c

2.07 a

2.08 i

2.09 e

2.010 n

2.011 f

2.012 o

2.013 b

2.014 k

2.015 g

2.016 true

2.017 false

2.018 true

2.019 true

2.020 true

2.021 false

2.022 false

2.023 true

2.024 b. gifts of healing

2.025 a. the Gentiles

2.026 d. was a major stumbling stone to the acceptance of the Gospel

2.027 c. 57-58

2.028 love

2.029 the body of Christ

2.030 Resurrection

2.031 of the house of Israel

2.032 16-17

2.033 Example:
One view insists on a particular set of scruples, and regards those who do not abide within these confines to be "liberalists." Those with a broader perspective find nothing sinful among the set of scruples, and label those who abide by them as "legalists." Paul promoted a more comprehensive view which calls upon each person's conscience and convictions, allowing others the same freedom. Paul understood that each person answers to God for himself.

2.034 a. Romans 1:1-1:17 Salutations
b. Romans 1:18-2:29 Downward spiral of sin
c. Romans 3 Universal sin and guilt, with emphasis on Jews
d. Romans 4 Abraham
e. Romans 5 Justification
f. Romans 6 Reckoning justification by baptism
g. Romans 7 Carnal nature vs. spiritual nature
h. Romans 8 Life in the Holy Spirit
i. Romans 9 God's sovereignty
j. Romans 10 Jewish unbelief
k. Romans 11 Grafting of the Gentiles
l. Romans 12 Dedication and service
m. Romans 13 Submission
n. Romans 14 Scruples
o. Romans 15 Unity
p. Romans 16 Salutations

SELF TEST 3

3.01 g

3.02 d

3.03 h

3.04 j

3.05 f

3.06 a or b

3.07 i

3.08 c

3.09 e or j

3.010 b

3.011 true

3.012 false

3.013 true

3.014 false

3.015 fulfillment

3.016 to receive Jesus as Savior

3.017 suffering or hard times

3.018 Phoebe

3.019 ministers

3.020 a. Romans chapter 9 - God's sovereignty
b. Romans chapter 10 - Jewish unbelief
c. Romans chapter 11 - Grafting of the Gentiles
d. Romans chapter 12 - Dedication and service
e. Romans chapter 13 - Submission
f. Romans chapter 14 - Scruples
g. Romans chapter 15 - Unity
h. Romans chapter 16 - Salutations

3.021 "The Spirit itself beareth witness with our spirit, that we are the children of God."

3.022 "That if thou shalt confess with thy mouth the Lord Jesus, and shalt believe in thine heart that God hath raised him from the dead, thou shalt be saved. For with the heart man believeth unto righteousness; and with the mouth confession is made unto salvation."

3.023 "For whosoever shall call upon the name of the Lord shall be saved."

3.024 "And we know that all things work together for good to them that love God, to them who are the called according to his purpose."

3.025 "He that spared not his own son, but delivered him up for us all, how shall he not with him also freely give us all things."

3.026 "But put ye on the Lord Jesus Christ, and make not provision for the flesh, to fulfil the lusts thereof."

3.027 "Nay, in all these things we are more than conquerors through him that loved us."

3.028 "So then faith cometh by hearing, and hearing by the word of God."

3.029 "I beseech you therefore, brethren, by the mercies of God, that ye present your bodies a living sacrifice, holy, acceptable unto God, which is your reasonable service. And be not conformed to this world: but be ye transformed by the renewing of your mind, that ye may prove what is that good, and acceptable, and perfect, will of God."

1.01   f

1.02   h

1.03   l

1.04   j

1.05   b

1.06   m

1.07   a

1.08   d

1.09   k

1.010 **g or e**

1.011 e

1.012 c

1.013 true

1.014 true

1.015 false

1.016 true

1.017 false

1.018 true

1.019 true

1.020 false

1.021 false

1.022 true

1.023 false

1.024 true

1.025 false

1.026 true

1.027 true

1.028 false

1.029 d

1.030 c

1.031 a

1.032 d

1.033 b

1.034 c

1.035 a

1.036 c

1.037 the Bible

1.038 prophets

1.039 name

1.040 Joshua

1.041 glory

1.042 sinless

1.043 He limited their independent
       useage. He performed miracles
       only on certain occasions. *example —*
       satan tempted Jesus in the
       wilderness.

SELF TEST 2

2.01   e

2.02   j

2.03   h

2.04   m

2.05   b

2.06   k

2.07   c

2.08   d

2.09   n

2.010   a

2.011   f

2.012   g

2.013   i

2.014   true

2.015   false

2.016   false

2.017   false

2.018   false

2.019   false

2.020   true

2.021   false

2.022   false

2.023   true

2.024   true

2.025   b

2.026   d

2.027   d

2.028   c

2.029   d

2.030   c

2.031   b

2.032   a.   person
        b.   work

2.033   a.   prophet
        b.   priest

2.034   miracles

2.035   a.   redemption
        b.   a ransom

2.036   a.   human nature
        b.   divine nature

2.037   he was a spirit

2.038   Either order:
        a.   its immortality
        b.   not being subject to the physical
             laws of nature

2.039   a.   Ascension
        b.   Incarnation

2.040   His humanity and deity give Him
        understanding of both sides. His
        presence in heaven enables Him
        to represent us in God's presence.

SELF TEST 1

1.01   f

1.02   j

1.03   t

1.04   o

1.05   h

1.06   d

1.07   c

1.08   k

1.09   s

1.010   n

1.011   a

1.012   i

1.013   r

1.014   e

1.015   q

1.016   b

1.017   l

1.018   g

1.019   p

1.020   m

1.021   c. green garden land

1.022   b. gratuitous

1.023   a. Goshen

1.024   d. Cyrus

1.025   b. 400

1.026   father of a nation

1.027   Ur

1.028   covenant

1.029   Saul

1.030   high priests

1.031   Alexander the Great

1.032   Septuagint

1.033   Antiochus Ephiphanes

1.034   the hammer

1.035   Roman Empire

1.036   the scattering of the Jews after the Babylon exile

1.037   a person who has been converted from one religion, opinion, or party to another

1.038   Example:
Jewish rejection of their Messiah opened the door whereby Gentiles could hear and believe the gospel.

1.039   Example:
In each country of his empire he founded a model city, erecting public buildings, gymnasiums, theaters, and so forth and encouraged individuals to adopt Hellenistic lifestyles.

SELF TEST 2

2.01   f

2.02   g

2.03   k

2.04   j

2.05   n

2.06   s

2.07   c

159

2.08   d

2.09   p

2.010   m

2.011   t

2.012   b

2.013   i

2.014   r

2.015   q or u

2.016   a

2.017   l

2.018   e

2.019   o

2.020   h

2.021   true

2.022   false

2.023   false

2.024   true

2.025   false

2.026   true

2.027   false

2.028   false

2.029   true

2.030   true

2.031   b. 606

2.032   c. Rehoboam

2.033   a. Bethlehem

2.034   c. Septuagint

2.035   d. Alexander the Great

2.036   b. 1939 to 1945

2.037   d. Europe

2.038   b. Jesus

2.039   a. city

2.040   c. French

2.041   Mattathias

2.042   Diaspora

2.043   Byzantium

2.044   Moses Mendelssohn

2.045   crusaders

2.046   Saviour

2.047   Gentile

2.048   Jesus Christ

2.049   Jews

2.050   Islam

2.051   a. Persian Empire
        b. Alexander the Great's Empire
        c. Seleucid and Ptolemaic Empires
        d. Maccabean period
        e. Roman Empire

2.052   Example; should include these main
        points:
        When the Syrians took control of
        Palestine, they were determined to
        enforce Hellenism upon the Jews.
        The Jews who favored the Greek life
        style became opposed to the orthodox
        Jews, especially concerning the
        office of high priest. Antiochus
        Epiphanes used this rivalry as an
        opportunity to destroy orthodox
        Judaism. He erected a statue of
        Jupiter in the Temple, and used
        swine for sacrifice. He also for-
        bade the Jews to worship on the
        Sabbath, practice circumcision, or
        observe the feast days. Copies of
        the Scriptures were destroyed and
        Jewish people were sold as slaves,
        beaten, or killed. Finally an aged
        priest named Mattathias, along with
        his five sons and some followers,
        arose in rebellion against the Syrians.

SELF TEST 3

3.01   o

3.02   j

3.03   r

3.04   l

3.05   u

3.06   a

3.07   p

3.08   k

3.09   f

3.010   q

3.011   i

3.012   c

3.013   n

3.014   t

3.015   m

3.016   d

3.017   e

3.018   b

3.019   h

3.020   g

3.021   true

3.022   true

3.023   false

3.024   false

3.025   true

3.026   true

3.027   true

3.028   false

3.029 true

3.030   false

3.031   father of a nation

3.032   Eliezer

3.033   Cyrus

3.034   Egypt

3.035   proselyte

3.036   Behistun Inscription

3.037   Jerusalem

3.038   Babylonians

3.039   Nuzi Tablets

3.040   Moabite Stone

3.041   Essenes

3.042   Corinth

3.043   Bethlehem

3.044   Amarna Letters

3.045   scroll of Isaiah

3.046   the beginning of Judah's exile into Babylon

3.047   Israel was exiled into Assyria

3.048   Jerusalem was destroyed

3.049   Hitler became Chancellor of the German Reich

3.050   Israel became a nation

3.051   Any order:
        a. get out of his country
        b. leave his kindred
        c. leave his father's house
        d. go to a land that God would show him

3.052   Example:
        A covenant is a binding and solemn agreement made by two or more parties in which each party agrees to certain conditions. In the making of the Abrahamic Covenant, the animals were cut in two. While Abraham was asleep, a smoking furnace and a burning lamp passed between the pieces.

SELF TEST 1

1.01   e

1.02   d

1.03   g

1.04   a

1.05   h

1.06   b

1.07   f

1.08   c

1.09   c. bribes

1.010   c. the Bible

1.011   d. reveals the Christ

1.012   a. God-breathed

1.013   b. battery

1.014   d. astrology

1.015   c. hidden

1.016   a. authority

1.017   fall

1.018   serpent

1.019   natural

1.020   God's Son

1.021   written

1.022   verbal

1.023   three

1.024   blindness

1.025   saith

1.026   redemption

1.027   one

1.028   broken

1.029   c

1.030   d

1.031   a

1.032   f

1.033   b

1.034   Either order:
        a. natural
        b. specific

1.035   Either order:
        a. living
        b. written

1.036   a. First, always keep in mind the central message of the whole Bible and God's purpose with specific revelation.
        b. Second, gain understanding of and appreciation for individual writers and their individual book.
        c. Third, complete your introductory studies to place the passage under study in its proper historical setting.
        d. Finally, compare your interpretation with other passages of Scripture that appear to address the same subject. In other words, compare Scripture with Scripture.

1.037   Specific revelation affords people the blessed privilege of knowing God, and knowing Him as their Creator God, their Savior God, and through Jesus, as their Heavenly Father. In Specific revelation, God shows people their need and introduces His Christ, Jesus, as their savior and champion. In Specific revelation, God lets people know how trusting in the person of Jesus, and believing in the work of Jesus changes their position and their destiny immediately and for all eternity.

SELF TEST 2

2.01   e

2.02   g

2.03   a

2.04   h

2.05   b

2.06   c

2.07   d

2.08   j

2.09   f

2.010   i

2.011   b. patriarch

2.012   a. The Torah

2.013   c. phonogram

2.014   a. ideograph

2.015   c. pictograph

2.016   b. Thessalonica

2.017   d. The Five Rolls

2.018   c. Moses

2.019   b. Theophilus

2.020   c. Peter

2.021   wrote

2.022   society

2.023   1440 B.C.

2.024   Moses

2.025   587 B.C.

2.026   thousand

2.027   Latter Prophets

2.028   James

2.029   Hebrews

2.030   a. First, what was the message to the original readership or audience?
        b. Second, what does this message teach with respect to the Messiah's advent---- his first coming as a babe in a manger.
        c. Third, what does this message show us with respect to Christ's second coming as returning, ruling King?

2.031   And I will put enmity between thee [serpent] and the woman, and between thy seed and her seed; it shall bruise thy head, and thou shalt bruise his heel.

2.032   Job, like the patriarchs, clearly functions as a spiritual leader within his household. In fact, he serves as a mediator, or priest, for his family (see Job 1:5). So Job lived before the establishment in Moses' era of a formal order of priests. Similarly, Job must have lived prior to the construction of the tabernacle and establishment of sacrificial worship. Other scriptures do attest that Job was a real historical figure (Ezekiel 14:14-20 and James 5:11). Apparently, Moses wrote down a story that had been preserved in the oral tradition of Abraham's descendants.

2.033   About 250 B.C., the Jewish leaders in Alexandria, Egypt recognized that cultural and economic pressures were forcing young Jews to live and work in a Hellenized (Greek) culture using the Greek language. Young people became less and less familiar with Hebrew and could not read and understand the Holy Scriptures. Out of concern that the Scriptures would no longer function as a guide for faith and life among Hellenized Jews, the leaders commissioned seventy scholars to translate the Hebrew Scriptures into Greek. This translation of the seventy Hebrew-Greek scholars came to be known as the Septuagint. This Work restored the Holy Scriptures to a place of authority and influence in the Greek speaking Jewish community. Greek uses vowels, Hebrew doesn't, so the text was a lot longer. The translators added a fourth division to the Hebrew Old Testament: Law, Prophets, Writings and Poetical books.

SELF TEST 3

3.01   c

3.02   d

3.03   i

3.04   g

3.05   a

3.06   b

3.07   e

3.08   j

3.09   f

3.010   h

3.011   b. Samuel

3.012   c. Habakkuk

3.013   a. Rabbis

3.014   b. Constantine

3.015   d. Apocrypha

3.016   b. Pseudepigrapha

3.017   a. Clement of Rome

3.018   c. Irenaeus

3.019   d. Eusebius

3.020   c. A.D. 419

3.021   Christ

3.022   seventy

3.023   messianic

3.024   pseudepigrapha

3.025   apocrypha

3.026   Nicaea

3.027   Any order:
a. Were the books recognized immediately, and also later, as being inspired by God?
b. Were the books received by God's people initially, as well as later, as Holy Scripture?
c. Were the books regularly preserved and collected by God's people?

3.028   Either order:
a. Were the authors prophets, that is, did each author serve in the office of prophet; and/or did the author possess the spiritual gift of prophecy?
b. Were the writings historically and prophetically accurate?

3.029   Any three of the following six:
a. Did the writing include a claim to inspiration?
b. Was the writing by one of the Apostles or his delegate?
c. Was the writing received by the churches?
d. Was the writing consistent with other inspired works?
e. Did the original recipients recognize the writing as being from God?
f. Did the writing contain directives for public circulation and use?

3.030   Either order:
a. serious re-examination of certain books or questions in light of archeological discoveries of ancient texts
b. questions rooted in the cynicism, skepticism and unbelief of people who are anti-Christianity, anti-Christ and anti-God

3.031   Either order:
a. no other canonical authors or books include any citations or quotations from any of these writings.
b. doctrines that are inconsistent with or contradictory to that taught in the canon are put forward in the Apocryphal writings.

3.032   When a prophet speaketh in the name of the LORD, if the thing follow not, nor come to pass, that is the thing which the LORD hath not spoken, but the prophet hath spoken it presumptuously: thou shalt not be afraid of him.

1.01   c

1.02   e

1.03   f

1.04   a

1.05   d

1.06   b

1.07   i

1.08   g

1.09   j

1.010   h

1.011   false

1.012   **true**

1.013   true

1.014   **true**

1.015   true

1.016   false

1.017   true

1.018   true

1.019   true

1.020   true

1.021   c. counsel

1.022   a. Exodus 33:11

1.023   d. Mephiboseth

1.024   d. a, b, and c

1.025   a. John chapter 15

1.026   c. 1 Corinthians   chapter 13

1.027   c. an outcast

1.028   b. stranger

1.029   **d. my brethren**

1.030   they be agreed

1.031   a brother (relative)

1.032   ye do whatsoever I command you

1.033   that a man **lay down his life for his friends**

1.034   ye have love one to another

1.035   **thy neighbour as thyself**

1.036   publicans and sinners

1.037   corrupts good manner

1.038   consent thou not

1.039   mercy

1.040   **Any order:**
a. he loves
b. is unchanging
c. is honest with us
or is closer than a brother,
a comrade, a helper, a
counselor and so on

1.041   Abraham

1.042   Any order:
a. love
b. obedience
c. maturity
   or self-denial

SELF TEST 2

2.01   f

2.02   a

2.03   g

2.04   d

2.05   b

2.06   h

2.07   i

2.08   j

2.09   c

2.010   e

2.011   true

2.012   false

2.013   true

2.014   false

2.015   true

2.016   false

2.017   true

2.018   true

2.019   false

2.020   true

2.021   c. an outcast

2.022   b. stranger

2.023   **d. my brethren**

2.024   c. leadership

2.025   d. a, b, and c

2.026   d. a, b, and c

2.027   d. neither a, b, nor c

2.028   d. a, b, and c

2.029   d. a, b, and c

2.030   d. a, b, and c

2.031   **that a man lay down his life**
        for his friends

2.032   corrupt   good manners

2.033   brother

2.034   transformed by the renewing of
        your mind

2.035   **we may be accepted of Him**

2.036   in all manner of conversation

2.037   **that shall he also reap**

2.038   his good to edification

2.039   **shall not fulfill the lust of the**
        flesh

2.040   **with all purity**

2.041   Any order:
        a. To please the Lord
        b. Not to please ourself
        c. Walk in the Spirit

2.042   Any order:
        a. a relationship to the opposite
           sex
        b. an expression of masculine
           initiative
        c. a prearranged agreement
        d. a parental consent and blessing
        e. a participation in a social
           engagement
        f. a thoughtful and considered plan

SELF TEST 3

3.01   d

3.02   g

3.03   a

3.04   j

3.05   b

3.06   c

3.07   e

3.08   i

3.09   f

3.010   h

3.011   false

3.012   true

3.013   false

3.014   true

3.015   true

3.016   false

3.017   true

3.018   false

3.019   false

3.020   true

3.021   d. ungodly

3.022   d. Mephibosheth

3.023   c. 1 Corinthians Chapter 13

3.024   c. leadership

3.025   d. a, b, and c

3.026   d. neither a, b, nor c

3.027   d. a, b, and c

3.028   d. a, b, and c

3.029   c. executed

3.030   d. a, b, and c

3.031   ye do whatsoever I command you

3.032   corrupt good manners

3.033   that a man lay down his life for his friends

3.034   a brother

3.035   that shall he also reap

3.036   in all manner of conservation

3.037   with all purity

3.038   shall not fulfill the lust of the flesh

3.039   they shall be one flesh

3.040   neither marry nor are given in marriage

3.041   Any order:
        a. loveth at all times
        b. sticks closer than a brother
        c. hearty counsel

3.042   Any order:
        a. lay down ones life
        b. obedience
        c. sharing what has been given you

3.043   Any order:
        a. a relationship to the opposite sex
        b. an expression of masculine initiative
        c. a prearranged agreement
        d. parental consent and blessing
        e. a participation in social engagement
        f. a thoughtful and considered plan

Self Test 1

1.01	d
1.02	h
1.03	e
1.04	a
1.05	f
1.06	b
1.07	g
1.08	5
1.09	1
1.010	6
1.011	3
1.012	2
1.013	4
1.014	7
1.015	anoint
1.016	remnant
1.017	unconditional
1.018	concubine
1.019	Succession
1.020	false
1.021	true
1.022	true
1.023	false
1.024	false
1.025	true
1.026	true
1.027	false
1.028	true
1.029	true
1.030	false
1.031	true

1.032   Suggested answers:

a. Answers may include that he advised his son on the importance of following God's law. He also warned Solomon of some of the threats to his throne. David served alongside his son for a number of months. David also served as a role model for his son.

b. Answers may include that generally the priest anointed the next king in a regular succession. Prophets anointed the king when the typical order of succession was not followed. Prophets also addressed the sins of the king and others in the kingdom.

Self Test 2

2.01	k
2.02	g
2.03	h
2.04	i
2.05	e
2.06	f
2.07	b
2.08	d
2.09	c
2.010	j
2.011	a
2.012	true

2.013   false

2.014   false

2.015   false

2.016   true

2.017   false

2.018   false

2.019   false

2.020   true

2.021   false

2.022   true

2.023   true

2.024   false

2.025   true

2.026   c

2.027   b

2.028   a

2.029   b

2.030   b

2.031   c

2.032   a

2.033   b

2.034   a

2.035   c

2.036   c

2.037   b

2.038   discernment

2.039   affiliation

2.040   pestilence

2.041   animosity

2.042   deter

2.043   memorabilia

2.044   conscripted

2.045   accolades

2.046   Suggested answers:

a. Students should remember that Solomon's gift of wisdom brought him discernment as he ruled the people. He was able to use his intellect to assist him in building the temple in Jerusalem. Solomon's wisdom also brought peace to the kingdom and freedom from oppression from foreign leaders. Unfortunately Solomon's wisdom brought with it pride in his own abilities. Solomon was drawn in by his foreign wives and served other gods. Solomon's sinful choices diminished God's good gift of wisdom.

b. Answers should include that one of the ways in which Solomon brought peace to Israel was through treaties with foreign leaders. As a sign of their loyalty, these leaders offered their daughters in marriage to Israel's kings. These women brought with them their gods and traditions. Solomon would eventually serve these gods. As a result, Israel began to experience both internal and external strife. After Solomon's death, the kingdom would be divided and never again be united under one king.

Self Test 3

3.01   d

3.02   j

3.03	c
3.04	b
3.05	g
3.06	f
3.07	e
3.08	i
3.09	h
3.010	a
3.011	c, a
3.012	c
3.013	a
3.014	b
3.015	b
3.016	c
3.017	b
3.018	b
3.019	c
3.020	a
3.021	secular
3.022	thesis
3.023	diatribe
3.024	capricious
3.025	dog tag
3.026	counterpoint
3.027	reiterating
3.028	resolution
3.029	false
3.030	true

3.031	false
3.032	true
3.033	false
3.034	false
3.035	false
3.036	true
3.037	true
3.038	true

3.039   Suggested answers:

a. Solomon used the phrase "vanity of vanities" to refer to the hopelessness and meaninglessness of life. He began the book of Ecclesiastes speaking of his quest to find meaning in life. Throughout the book he repeated the phrase "under the sun" which referred to life on earth and the period of a person's life. Students should include an understanding of the meaning of the phrases as well as the theme of the book in their answers.

b. When Solomon obeyed God and followed his law, God blessed him and his kingdom. He was able to expand Israel's borders and strengthen his kingdom from outside threats. Solomon also built and dedicated a temple to God. When Solomon turned from God's ways, his life and that of his kingdom deteriorated. Solomon began worshipping foreign gods and Jeroboam threatened his rule. As students reflect on their own lives, they should include references to God's law in general as well as specific commands. Their answers on how they obey and disobey God's laws will differ.

SELF TEST 1

1.01   d

1.02   h

1.03   g

1.04   j

1.05   a

1.06   i

1.07   k

1.08   b

1.09   e

1.010   c

1.011   false

1.012   true

1.013   true

1.014   true

1.015   true

1.016   false

1.017   false

1.018   true

1.019   true

1.020   false

1.021   d

1.022   d

1.023   c

1.024   b

1.025   a

1.026   b

1.027   c

1.028   a

1.029   c

1.030   d

1.031   fool

1.032   backgrounds

1.033   Luke

1.034   numbers

1.035   poetic

1.036   translated

1.037   physiological

1.038   botany

1.039   astronomy

1.040   geology

1.041   **Any order:**
a.   ethical variances
b.   doctrinal variances
c.   numerical variances
d.   factual variances
e.   parallel passages

1.042   Example:
He should not ignore them, but neither should he disbelieve the Bible.

1.043   Example:
He should trust God's Word, examine problem passages, and either reach a conclusion or suspend judgment.

SELF TEST 2

2.01   e

2.02   i

2.03   k

2.04   j

2.05   h

2.06   g

2.07   a

2.08   c

2.09   f

2.010   d

2.011   d

2.012   c

2.013   a

2.014   b

2.015   d

2.016   d

2.017   d

2.018   b

2.019   d

2.020   c

2.021   true

2.022   true

2.023   false

2.024   false

2.025   true

2.026   true

2.027   true

2.028   true

2.029   false

2.030   false

2.031   fool

2.032   poetic

2.033   less

2.034   Incarnate

2.035   God

2.036   child's

2.037   clues or indicators

2.038   darkness

2.039   upward

2.040   dump

2.041   Any order:
a. "All religions contain some truth."
b. "All roads lead to Rome."
c. "Good, sincere people are in all religions."

2.042   Any order:
a. It follows the authentic Word of God, not the teachings of men.
b. Its God is a Trinity, not a simple deity.
c. It has a resurrected Saviour, not a dead founder.
d. It offers salvation by grace, not works.

2.043   Any order:
a. power
b. patience
c. justice
d. holiness
e. grace
f. love

2.044   Any order:
a. Nature reveals God.
b. Men rejected God when they knew Him.
c. Men prefer sin to God.

SELF TEST 3

3.01   true

3.02   false

3.03   false

3.04   true

3.05   false

3.06   true

3.07   false

3.08   false

3.09   true

3.010   true

3.011   contrasting

3.012   humanity

3.013   limits

3.014   prayers

3.015   grace

3.016   Holy Spirit

3.017   a. outward
        b. inward

3.018   faith

3.019   activities

3.020   f

3.021   c

3.022   h

3.023   b

3.024   i

3.025   a

3.026   d

3.027   g

3.028   e

3.029   k

3.030   Any order:
      a. saving relationship
      b. believing relationship
      c. yielding relationship
      d. obeying relationship
      e. continuing relationship

3.031   Any order:
      a. to correct our sin
      b. to teach obedience
      c. to turn from sin
      d. to cause us to mature spiritually
      e. to learn to depend on God
         or to glorify God

3.032   a. verifies a divine power
      or cause-and-effect
      b. verifies a divine intelligence
      or the orderly design and purpose
      of nature
      c. verifies a moral power
      or the analogy between man and
      his Creator

3.033   Any order:
      a. It follows the authentic Word
         of God rather than the
         teaching of men.
      b. Its God is a Trinity rather
         than a simple deity.
      c. It has a resurrected Saviour
         rather than a dead founder.
      d. It offers salvation by grace
         rather than works.

3.034   c

3.035   a

3.036   b

3.037   d

3.038   d

BIBLE 1110

SELF TEST 1

1.01   m

1.02   g

1.03   f

1.04   h

1.05   k

1.06   b

1.07   c

1.08   i

1.09   e

1.010   p

1.011   d

1.012   j

1.013   l

1.014   o

1.015   n

1.016   a. sixty-six
         b. fifteen

1.017   Either order:
         a. natural
         b. specific

1.018   hermeneutics

1.019   Jews

1.020   Babylonian Captivity

1.021   Any order:
         a. nature
         b. man's conscience
         c. The Bible, God's Word

1.022   Any order:
         a. The Torah
         b. The Prophets
         c. The Writings

1.023   Any order:
         a. Is it prophetic?
         b. Is it authoritative?
         c. Is it dynamic?
         or Is it authentic? or Was it
         received by God's people?

1.024   true

1.025   true

1.026   true

1.027   false

1.028   false

1.029   Example:
The Bible is the complete and final
message of salvation in Christ and
allows man to have a personal
relationship with God through
Jesus Christ.
or
The people of Israel had grown
to be a large nation and needed
a record of laws and regulations.

1.030   Example:
So that man could reach the point
where he could compose God's Word
in written form and Israel could
emerge as a nation.

1.031   Certain doctrinal differences with
the recognized canon made the
Apocrypha unacceptable. For
instance, II Maccabees mentions
prayers and offerings made on
behalf of dead saints.

1.032   Example:
It provided modern man and
archaeologists with the oldest extant
Old Testament manuscripts.

SELF TEST 2

2.01   d

2.02   j

2.03   f

2.04   e

2.05   i

2.06   c

2.07   k

2.08   b

2.09   g

2.010 l

2.011 h

2.012 m

2.013 n

2.014 o

2.015 a

2.016 Either order:
       a. natural
       b. specific

2.017 Resurrection

2.018 condemnation

2.019 senatorial aristocracy

2.020 Judaizers

2.021 faith

2.022 Pentateuch or Law, Torah

2.023 false

2.024 false

2.025 true

2.026 true

2.027 true

2.028 Jewish

2.029 a. Grafting
       b. Gentiles

2.030 a. Greetings
       b. Doxology

2.031 Example:
       Because of sin, man falls short
       of the glory of God. On his own
       efforts man will never reach God.
       Sin causes spiritual separation
       from God.

2.032 Example:
       God waited until man had the
       sufficient tools with which to
       record God's Word. He also waited
       until the nation of Israel had
       emerged.

2.033 Example:
       God looks at those in Christ Jesus
       as being identified with His Son.

2.034 Example:
       They become filled with all types
       of unrighteousness and become
       haters of God. They become worthy
       of death.

2.035 Example:
       These verses teach us that we have
       been justified by faith and that
       God loved us even though we were
       sinners. We now have peace with
       God through Jesus Christ.

SELF TEST 3

3.01   j

3.02   o

3.03   k

3.04   l

3.05   b

3.06   a

3.07   e

3.08   f

3.09   g

3.010 m

3.011 h

3.012 n

3.013   d

3.014   c

3.015   i

3.016   true

3.017   true

3.018   false

3.019   true

3.020   false

3.021   a.   1
        b.   16-17

3.022   400

3.023   covenant

3.024   Saul

3.025   a.   Cyrus
        b.   536

3.026   orally

3.027   Either order:
        a.   God waited until man could
             easily record His Word in
             written form.
        b.   He waited until Israel had
             emerged as a nation.

3.028   Any order:
        a.   The Torah (Law)
        b.   The Prophets
        c.   The Writings

3.029   Any order:
        a.   Saul
        b.   David
        c.   Solomon

3.030   Example:
        The normal way allowed to know
        things about Himself that otherwise
        would have been unknown. The
        specific revelations culminated with
        the birth of Christ, the Savior, who
        delivered man from sin.

3.031   Example:
        Five animals (except the birds)
        were cut in two. A smoking
        furnace and a burning lamp passed
        between the pieces while Abraham
        slept.

3.032   Example:
        The Jews experienced persecution,
        intolerance, and they suffered
        through the People's Crusade.
        They were under the influence of
        the Christians, Moslems, and the
        Byzantine Empire.

3.033   Example:
        The persecution of the Jews,
        destruction of copies of the
        Scriptures, and attempted destruc-
        tion of the orthodox Jewish faith
        by the Syrian ruler Antiochus
        Epiphanes.

SELF TEST 4

4.01   h

4.02   p

4.03   q

4.04   k

4.05   l

4.06   c

4.07   d

4.08   j

4.09   e

4.010   f

4.011   m

4.012   o

4.013   n

4.014   i

4.015   g

4.016   true

4.017   true

4.018   false

4.019   false

4.020   Abraham

4.021   a. carnal
        b. spiritual
        c. 7

4.022   faithfulness or parallels

4.023   attritubutes

4.024   Any order:
        a. Mediator between man and God
        b. man's Advocate
        c. man's Ambassador in heaven
        or man's Intercessor before God
            man's High Priest in heaven

4.025   Any order:
        a. The Torah (Law)
        b. The Prophets
        c. The Writings

4.026   Romans 1:16-17

4.027   "For I am not ashamed of the gospel
        of Christ: for it is the power of
        God unto salvation to every one
        that believeth; to the Jew first,
        and also to the Greek. For there-
        in is the righteousness of God
        revealed from faith to faith: as
        it is written, The just shall live
        by faith."

4.028   Example:
        when He died a sacrificial death on
        the cross for man

4.029   Example:
        a binding or solemn agreement
        between two or more parties

4.030   so that the way of salvation would
        be opened to the Gentiles

SELF TEST 5

5.01   p

5.02   o

5.03   e

5.04   d

5.05   a

5.06   k

5.07   f

5.08   g

5.09   c

5.010   q

5.011   h

5.012   i

5.013   j

5.014   l

5.015   m

5.016   n

5.017   true

5.018   true

5.019   true

5.020   true

5.021   a. Jews
        b. Septuagint

5.022   Romans 1:16-17

5.023   a.   search
        b.   happiness
        c.   recovery

5.024   1947

5.025   Any order:
        a.   physical
        b.   social
        c.   interpersonal

5.026   Israel or Jews

5.027   the Bible, God's Word

5.028   Emmanuel

5.029   Any order:
        a.   pleasure
        b.   possessions
        c.   money
      or reputation, sex, prestige,
          building fancy constructions

5.030   **Example:**
Israel would have laws to guarantee individual freedom and national freedoms. The Torah would become Israel's constitution.

5.031   Example:
God gives us opportunities to share our faith that may not come again. Jesus came to seek and save the lost, and we should follow His example.

5.032   Example:
You cannot find happiness in temporal things. Only God can provide us with the perfect inner happiness.

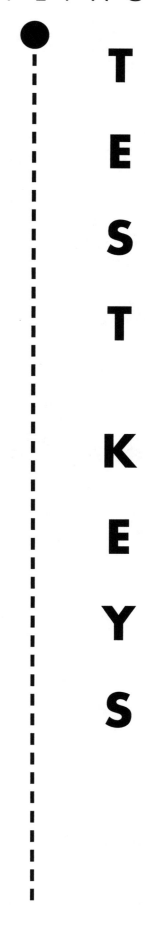

TEST KEYS

1. Any order:
    a. the affirmation of God's faithfulness
    b. the nature of God's faithfulness
    c. the manifestation of God's faithfulness
    d. the implications of God's faithfulness

2. Either order:
    a. immutability
    b. universality

3. It is perfect and absolutely trustworthy.

4. Either order:
    a. providential care of His creatures
    b. restoration promised to His creatures or gracious covenants

5. a steward of that grace

6. carelessness with the truth of God

7. Examples; any order:
    a. being persecuted for Christ's sake
    b. loving his enemies
    c. preaching the gospel willingly

8. a. His counsel
    b. His oath

9. They are man-made.

10. Example:
    They have never trusted in God, or
    They have no basis for faithfulness.

11. good Shepherd

12. promised Eve a Seed that would defeat Satan and redeem fallen man

13. He remains faithful.

14. Example:
    He is God, or He had perfect knowledge of God, or He perfectly obeyed God.

15. Aaron (Student could also correctly answer-Melchisedec)

16. Either order:
    a. His offering
    b. His intercession

17. Either order:
    a. God is the only credible object of faith.
    b. We must be faithful stewards.

18. Either order:
    a. not an owner
    b. must give an account

19. Either order:
    a. rewarded for one's own work
    b. only work that stands the fire will be rewarded

20. Either order:
    a. His Word
    b. His work

21. Either order:
    a. God's own testimony
    b. the testimonies of men who have trusted Him.

22. Examples; any order:
    a. Sinless
    b. Lives forever
    c. Makes man perfect
    d. Heavenly Tabernacle
    e. Offered only once

23. an attribute of God implying loyalty, constancy and freedom from arbitrariness and fickleness

24. Check against King James version of the Bible.

25. Check against King James version of the Bible.

26. Check against King James version of the Bible.

1. i
2. q
3. n
4. p
5. g
6. k
7. t
8. l
9. d
10. r
11. h
12. a
13. c
14. s
15. b
16. j
17. f
18. m
19. e
20. o
21. true
22. false
23. true
24. true
25. true
26. c
27. a

28. c
29. b
30. c
31. check on page 19 of LIFEPAC
32. Romans 1:1-1:17—Salutation
    Romans 1:18-2:29—Downward
      spiral of sin
    Romans 3—Universal sin and guilt
      with emphasis on Jewish nation
    Romans 4—Abraham
    Romans 5—Justification
    Romans 6—Reckoning
      justification by baptism
    Romans 7—Carnal nature vs.
      spiritual nature
    Romans 8—Life in the Holy Spirit

33. "For I am not ashamed of the gospel
    of Christ: for it is the power of
    God unto salvation to everyone that
    believeth; to the Jew first, and
    also to the Greek. For therein is
    the righteousness of God revealed
    from faith to faith: as it is
    written, The just shall live by
    faith."

34. "For all have sinned and come short
    of the glory of God."

35. "For the wages of sin is death; but
    the gift of God is eternal life
    through Jesus Christ our Lord. "

36. "Therefore being justified by faith,
    we have peace with God through our
    Lord Jesus Christ. "

37. "But God commendeth his love toward
    us, in that, while we were yet
    sinners, Christ died for us. "

38. "Likewise reckon ye also yourselves to
    be dead indeed unto sin, but alive
    unto God through Jesus Christ our Lord. "

39. "There is therefore now no condemnation
    to them which are in Christ Jesus,
    who walk not after the flesh but after
    the Spirit. "

1. j

2. h

3. n

4. l

5. i

6. a

7. m

8. c

9. o

10. e

11. b

12. d

13. f

14. k

15. g

16. true

17. false

18. true

19. false

20. faith

21. A.D. 57-58

22. letter bearer

23. Judaizers

24. repentance

25. circumcision

26. sovereignty

27. Gentiles

28. submit

29. the blood of the Lamb

30. d

31. i

32. a

33. g

34. e

35. b

36. f

37. c

38. "The Spirit itself beareth witness with our spirit, that we are the children of God."

39. "And we know that all things work together for good to them that love God, to them who are the called according to his purpose."

40. "Nay, in all these things we are more than conquerors through him that loved us."

41. "I beseech you therefore, brethren, by the mercies of God, that ye present your bodies a living sacrifice, holy, acceptable unto God, which is your reasonable service. And be not conformed to this world: but be ye transformed by the renewing of your mind, that ye may prove what is that good, and acceptable, and perfect will of God."

1. d
2. h
3. g
4. b
5. j
6. k
7. i
8. f
9. a
10. e
11. true
12. false
13. false
14. false
15. true
16. true
17. false
18. true
19. false
20. true
21. false
22. false
23. false
24. true

25. true
26. false
27. d
28. c
29. d
30. c
31. b
32. c
33. b
34. b
35. a
36. b
37. a
38. d
39. Peter
40. b. Son of man
41. a. High Priest
    b. tempted
    c. Advocate
42. teacher check

1. h

2. k

3. i

4. b

5. j

6. e

7. p

8. n

9. m

10. d

11. l

12. f

13. c

14. g

15. a

16. b. Rehoboam

17. c. Septuagint

18. a. New Amsterdam

19. c. the Tabernacle

20. d. Behistun Inscription

21. a. Ras Shamra Tablets

22. b. Ephesus

23. Isaac

24. judges

25. Byzantium

26. God the Father

27. Diaspora

28. Islam

29. Jeremiah

30. Mesha Stone

31. scroll of Isaiah

32. Capernaum

33. 2

34. 5

35. 1

36. 3

37. 4

38. c

39. a

40. f

41. b

42. e

1.	i	
2.	f	
3.	k	
4.	h	
5.	a	
6.	j	
7.	b	
8.	c	
9.	l	
10.	e	
11.	d	
12.	g	
13.	b.	the Bible
14.	a.	God-breathed
15.	a.	authority
16.	b.	patriarch
17.	c.	pictograph
18.	a.	Rabbis
19.	b.	Pseudepigrapha
20.	d.	Apocrypha
21.	d.	Eusebius
22.	b.	A.D. 419
23.	Creation	
24.	blindness	
25.	written	
26.	Latter Prophets	
27.	Christ	
28.	broken	
29.	Lord; pass; spoken; afraid	
30.	true	
31.	false	

32. true
33. false
34. true
35. false
36. true
37. false
38. true
39. true
40. true
41. Natural revelation reveals that God exists, that He is sovereign and powerful; and can, through human conscience, convict people when doing harm and wrong, and cause them to long for justic and truth.

42. Specific revelation affords people the blessed privilege of knowing God, and knowing Him as their Creator God, their Savior God, and through Jesus, as their Heavenly Father. In specific revelation, God lets people know how trusting in the person of Jesus, and believing in the work of Jesus changes their position and their destiny immediately and for all eternity.

43. Study to shew thyself approved unto God, a workman that needeth not to be ashamed, rightly dividing the word of truth.

1. c

2. i

3. f

4. a

5. j

6. b

7. h

8. g

9. e

10. d

11. false

12. false

13. true

14. true

15. true

16. false

17. false

18. true

19. true

20. true

21. c

22. b

23. d

24. c

25. b

26. d

27. d

28. d

29. d

30. d

31. corrupt good manners

32. consent thou not

33. mercy

34. in all manner of conversation

35. his good, to edification

36. shall not fulfill the lust of
    the flesh

37. with all purity

38. they shall be one flesh

39. neither marry nor are given in
    marriage

40. make an help meet for him

41. Any order; any three:
    a. loveth at all times
    b. sticketh closer than a brother
    c. hearty counsel
       or unchanging, honest,
       a helper, and so on

42. Any order:
    a. lay down ones life
    b. obedience
    c. sharing what has been given

43. Any order:
    a. please Him
    b. never please yourself (your neighbor)
    c. walk in the Spirit

1.	h		29.	true
2.	e		30.	secular
3.	i		31.	anoint
4.	g		32.	consolidating
5.	b		33.	deterrent
6.	c		34.	accolade
7.	j		35.	conscripted
8.	d		36.	discernment
9.	f		37.	memorabilia
10.	a		38.	concubines
11.	e		39.	remnant
12.	a		40.	pestilence
13.	b		41.	capricious
14.	g		42.	infrastructure
15.	c		43.	commodities
16.	d		44.	succession
17.	f		45.	3
18.	true		46.	8
19.	false		47.	4
20.	false		48.	7
21.	false		49.	2
22.	true		50.	1
23.	true		51.	5
24.	false		52.	6
25.	false		53.	b
26.	true		54.	a
27.	true		55.	c
28.	true		56.	b

57. b

58. a

59. c

60. c

61. Suggested answers:

a. Answers should include the advice
    David gave Solomon before his death
    as well as God's instructions to
    Solomon at Gibeon when God granted
    Solomon wisdom. David advised
    Solomon in both general and specific
    ways on how to rule the kingdom.
    Israel was safe from internal and
    external strength Israel when Solomon
    obeyed God's instructions as well as
    David's. Students should recall the
    wisdom with which Solomon ruled
    and his reliance on God's will and not
    his own. Students may make reference
    to the building of the temple and how
    at the dedication God's glory filled it.
    Solomon disobeyed God when he took
    foreign wives and accumulated
    wealth. He turned to the gods of other
    nations rather than the one, true God.
    Solomon began to face internal threats
    from Jeroboam. Solomon also began
    to have foreign kings attack Israel's
    borders.

b. There are a wide variety of ways
    students can approach this question.
    Students may focus on the limitless
    wisdom and knowledge of God as
    opposed to the finite wisdom of
    people. Students could also look at
    specific examples of how people
    behave when they follow God's ways.
    These would stand in contrast to
    people's pursuits when they follow
    what the world seems to think is
    important. As you evaluate students'
    answers, check to make sure that they
    include examples of both of God's
    wisdom and that of the world.

1. b

2. a

3. c

4. d

5. c

6. a

7. c

8. a

9. b

10. **c**

11. true

12. false

13. true

14. true

15. true

16. true

17. true

18. false

19. true

20. false

21. constructive

22. **unique or different**

23. suffering

24. yielding

25. Ararat

26. a. outward
    b. inward

27. God

28. a. numerical
    b. alleged contradictions

29. accuracy

30. incarnate

31. f

32. c

33. h

34. b

35. i

36. a

37. d

38. g

39. e

40. k

41. Any order:
    a. power
    b. patience
    c. justice
    d. holiness
    e. grace
    f. love

42. The age at which a child becomes aware of his sin

43. The Bible gives us clues that heaven is upward, and hell is downward toward the core of the earth.

44. Example:
    He should not ignore them, but neither should he disbelieve the Bible.

45. Example:
    He should trust God's Word, examine problem passages, and either reach a conclusion or suspend judgment.

1. l

2. f

3. b

4. d

5. j

6. o

7. g

8. e

9. i

10. h

11. k

12. p

13. n

14. m

15. a

16. true

17. true

18. false

19. true

20. true

21. a. Chaldea
    b. nation

22. Rosetta Stone

23. twentieth

24. a. complement or woman
    b. managing or filling

25. a. veiled
    b. limited

26. Any order:
    a. to establish doctrines of salvation
    b. to fortify Romans against the Judaizers
    c. to explain the unbelief of Israel and the relationship of Jews and Gentiles in the church
    or to urge Romans to maturity; to reveal to the Romans their relationship to each other and the government; to send personal greetings

27. a. Life
    b. sovereignty
    c. Israel's
    d. 11
    e. Gentiles

28. Any order:
    a. land
    b. blessing
    c. a nation

29. Example:
    Christians should view the Bible as the high and holy book it is. On its pages is the record of God's activity among men and the offer of eternal life in the person of the Lord Jesus.

30. Example:
    The Bible offers all that a person needs for life and acceptability with God. It is God's record of righteousness by faith and God's instrument for completing a life of faith.

TESTS

1. false

2. false

3. true

4. false

5. true

6. c

7. a

8. d

9. e

10. b

11. witnesses

12. forsake

13. Shepherd

14. gods

15. conditional

16. everlasting

17. Either order:
    a. God
    b. man

18. a. priesthood
    b. priesthood

19. intercession

20. God

21. He would not fail him nor forsake him.

22. "The gates of hell shall not prevail against it." (Matthew 16:18)

23. Either order:
    a. Baal could not hear.
    b. Baal could not speak.
    or Baal could not protect his property.
    or Baal was dead.

24. Any order:
    a. He makes us to lie down in green pastures.
    b. He restores our souls.
    c. He leads us in paths of righteousness.
    or He leads us beside still waters.
    He is with us in the valley of death.
    He comforts us.
    He prepares a table for us in the presence of our enemies.
    He gives us eternal life in His house.

25. d

26. a

27. b

28. e

29. c

1. c

2. a

3. f

4. b

5. e

6. true

7. true

8. false

9. true

10. false

11. b

12. c

13. d

14. c

15. c

16. 57-58

17. Phoebe

18. sin

19. atonement

20. pantheism

21. Any order:
    a. Augustus
    b. Tiberius
    c. Caligula (Gaius)
    d. Claudius
    e. Nero

22. Examples:
    a. salvation
    b. downward spiral of sin
    c. universal sin and guilt, with emphasis on the Jewish nation
    d. Abraham
    e. justification
    f. reckoning justification by baptism
    g. carnal nature vs. spiritual nature
    h. life in the Holy Spirit

23. a. "For I am not ashamed of the gospel of Christ; for it is the power of God unto salvation to everyone that believeth; to the Jew first and also to the Greek. For therein is the righteousness of God revealed from faith to faith as it is written, the just shall live by faith."

    b. "For all have sinned and come short of the glory of God."

    c. "For the wages of sin is death, but the gift of God is eternal life through Jesus Christ our Lord."

    d. "Therefore being justified by faith, we have peace with God through our Lord Jesus Christ."

    e. "But God commendeth his love toward us, in that, while we were yet sinners, Christ died for us."

    f. "Likewise reckon yourselves dead indeed to sin, but alive unto God through Jesus Christ our Lord."

    g. "There is therefore now no condemnation to them which are in Christ Jesus, who walk not after the flesh but after the Spirit."

24. Example:
    The error was their belief that a person could not become a Christian without first becoming a Jewish proselyte. They believed only the circumcised were heirs of Abraham and entitled to God's promises. Paul used the example of Abraham to demonstrate that circumcision was a token of his faith which was counted to him as righteousness. Faith, not circumcision, is the instrument to justification through Jesus Christ.

1. e

2. g

3. a

4. i

5. h

6. c

7. j

8. b

9. d

10. d

11. true

12. true

13. true

14. false

15. false

16. b

17. c

18. d

19. a

20. c

21. c

22. d

23. c

24. b

25. a

26. **Any order** ; any five:
 a. prophecy
 b. ministry
 c. teaching
 d. exhorting
 e. giving
 f. ruling
 g. showing mercy

27. a. 9
 b. 6
 c. 4
 d. 15
 e. 3
 f. 7
 g. 14
 h. 5
 i. 13
 j. 11

28. "That if thou shalt confess with thy mouth the Lord Jesus, and shalt believe in thine heart that God hath raised him from the dead, thou shalt be saved. For with the heart man believeth unto righteousness; and with the mouth confession is made unto salvation."

29. "For whosoever shall call upon the name of the Lord shall be saved."

30. "He that spared not his own Son, but delivered him up for us all, how shall he not with him also freely give us all things."

31. "So then faith cometh by hearing, and hearing by the word of God."

1.	f	26.	d
2.	d	27.	a
3.	a	28.	b
4.	g	29.	c
5.	k	30.	d
6.	b	31.	d
7.	j	32.	c
8.	c	33.	d
9.	e	34.	a
10.	h	35.	c
11.	false	36.	b
12.	false	37.	d
13.	false	38.	the Bible
14.	false	39.	blood
15.	true	40.	substitution
16.	true	41.	See Isaiah 9:6, Mark 10:45, Luke 2:52, John 1:1, 1 Timothy 2:5, or 1 Peter 1:18 and 19.
17.	true		
18.	true		
19.	false		
20.	false		
21.	true		
22.	true		
23.	false		
24.	true		
25.	false		

1. g
2. o
3. j
4. b
5. m
6. c
7. f
8. n
9. e
10. q
11. i
12. r
13. h
14. p
15. k
16. t
17. a
18. s
19. d
20. l
21. false
22. true
23. true
24. false
25. false

26. Amarna Letters
27. Moabite Stone
28. *father of a nation*
29. Esther
30. Adolf Hitler
31. Napoleon
32. Moab
33. Jeroboam
34. Isaac
35. Rome
36. Six Day War
37. Israel falls to Assyrian king
38. Constantine becomes emperor of Rome
39. World War II
40. Rome destroys Jerusalem

1.	e	28.	Either order: a. freedom b. blessing
2.	f	29.	five thousand
3.	g	30.	nation
4.	a	31.	Either order: a. Major prophets b. Minor prophets
5.	b	32.	Septuagint
6.	j	33.	God-breathed
7.	c	34.	Hebrews
8.	i	35.	Either order: a. Roman Catholic b. Eastern Orthodox
9.	d	36.	thank; Word; God; believe
10.	h	37.	speaketh; follow; not; afraid
11.	false	38.	inspired; profitable; righteousness
12.	true	39.	enmity; seed; head
13.	false		
14.	false		
15.	true		
16.	false		
17.	true		
18.	false		
19.	true		
20.	true		
21.	b. the Bible		
22.	a. the Torah		
23.	c. Peter		
24.	b. Pseudepigrapha		
25.	c. Irenaeus		
26.	Either order: a. living b. written		
27.	theophany		

1. e

2. g

3. c

4. j

5. h

6. d

7. k

8. i

9. f

10. a

11. false

12. true

13. false

14. false

15. true

16. true

17. false

18. true

19. true

20. false

21. social

22. goals

23. Either order:
a. leave
b. cleave

24. a. Christ's
b. church

25. time

26. social

27. sanctified

28. husband

29. **virtuous**

30. subjection

31. head

32. Either order:
a. among those we know
b. among strangers

33. Either order:
a. being friendly
b. seeking friends

34. Any order:
a. be fruitful
b. multiply
c. replenish the earth
d. subdue the earth

35. Any order:
a. loves at all times
b. closer than a brother
c. a good counselor (or friend
in adversity)

1.	b		29.	2
2.	a		30.	6
3.	c		31.	1
4.	k		32.	5
5.	e		33.	false
6.	d		34.	true
7.	g		35.	true
8.	i		36.	true
9.	f		37.	false
10.	h		38.	false
11.	l		39.	true
12.	j		40.	false
13.	Absalom		41.	true
14.	Mount Moriah		42.	false
15.	Gibeon		43.	true
16.	Nathan		44.	true
17.	Tyre		45.	a
18.	David		46.	c
19.	high places		47.	c
20.	Adonijah		48.	b
21.	Queen of Sheba		49.	b
22.	Jeroboam		50.	c
23.	Euphrates		51.	a
24.	Rehoboam		52.	b
25.	8		53.	Suggested answers:
26.	3			
27.	4			a. Temptations Solomon faced include relying on his own wisdom, marrying foreign wives, and receiving praise from foreign leaders. Answers should include that Solomon began to depend
28.	7			

more on himself than God which led him into embracing the ways of the world rather than God's ways. Solomon started worshipping the idols of his wives instead of only God. Temptations Christians face today may include pursing wealth, possessions, and entertainments instead of God. Students should reflect on how becoming caught up in earthly pursuits takes them away from spending time with God and following his commands.

b. Promises made to David included a member of his family ruling on Israel's throne forever and having his son build God's temple. Solomon built the temple David planned. Jesus, a descendant of David, would fulfill God's promise to have a member of his family rule on Israel's throne forever. Promises made to Solomon included granting him wisdom along with wealth and power if he obeyed God. God gave Solomon wisdom far greater than any other person. God also fulfilled his promise to give Solomon wealth and power when he obeyed and followed God's commands. Students may make the connection that God keeps his promises, but people do not.

1.	e	26.	c
2.	h	27.	b
3.	f	28.	a
4.	i	29.	d
5.	b	30.	d
6.	d	31.	a
7.	a	32.	numbers
8.	c	33.	worship
9.	g	34.	*persons*
10.	false	35.	blasphemy against the Holy Spirit
11.	true	36.	See 2 Timothy 3:16 and 17.
12.	false		
13.	false		
14.	true		
15.	false		
16.	false		
17.	true		
18.	false		
19.	false		
20.	b		
21.	c		
22.	a		
23.	b		
24.	d		
25.	d		

1. e

2. g

3. k

4. b

5. n

6. j

7. l

8. o

9. c

10. i

11. f

12. h

13. m

14. p

15. d

16. false

17. true

18. false

19. true

20. true

21. true

22. true

23. false

24. true

25. false

26. true

27. true

28. false

29. false

30. false

31. Jonathan

32. judgment

33. inspiration

34. Dead Sea Scrolls

35. emperors

36. Either order:
a. Rome
b. Spain

37. covenant

38. faithfulness

39. righteousness

40. 1948

41. Any order:
a. church fathers
b. apologists
c. theologians

42. Examples; any order:
a. Rosetta Stone
b. Behistum Inscription
c. City of Nuzi
d. Dead Sea Scrolls

43. Any order:
a. David
b. Solomon
c. Saul

44. Examples; any order:
a. Begin
b. Sadat
c. Carter